Cambridge Elements

Elements in Applied Evolutionary Science
edited by
David F. Bjorklund
Florida Atlantic University

EVOLUTION IN INTERNATIONAL RELATIONS

Jeremy Garlick
Prague University of Economics and Business

THE EVOLUTION INSTITUTE

Shaftesbury Road, Cambridge CB2 8EA, United Kingdom

One Liberty Plaza, 20th Floor, New York, NY 10006, USA

477 Williamstown Road, Port Melbourne, VIC 3207, Australia

314–321, 3rd Floor, Plot 3, Splendor Forum, Jasola District Centre, New Delhi – 110025, India

103 Penang Road, #05–06/07, Visioncrest Commercial, Singapore 238467

Cambridge University Press is part of Cambridge University Press & Assessment, a department of the University of Cambridge.

We share the University's mission to contribute to society through the pursuit of education, learning and research at the highest international levels of excellence.

www.cambridge.org
Information on this title: www.cambridge.org/9781009464161

DOI: 10.1017/9781009464154

© Jeremy Garlick 2025

This publication is in copyright. Subject to statutory exception and to the provisions of relevant collective licensing agreements, no reproduction of any part may take place without the written permission of Cambridge University Press & Assessment.

When citing this work, please include a reference to the DOI 10.1017/9781009464154

First published 2025

A catalogue record for this publication is available from the British Library

ISBN 978-1-009-46416-1 Hardback
ISBN 978-1-009-46414-7 Paperback
ISSN 2752-9428 (online)
ISSN 2752-941X (print)

Cambridge University Press & Assessment has no responsibility for the persistence or accuracy of URLs for external or third-party internet websites referred to in this publication and does not guarantee that any content on such websites is, or will remain, accurate or appropriate.

Evolution in International Relations

Elements in Applied Evolutionary Science

DOI: 10.1017/9781009464154
First published online: February 2025

Jeremy Garlick
Prague University of Economics and Business
Author for correspondence: Jeremy Garlick, jeremygarlick@yahoo.co.uk

Abstract: Scholars of international relations (IR) and evolution pay little attention to each other's fields. However, there is a need to examine evolution's impacts in IR. International actors such as nations are made up of people, so evolved human nature has an impact on relations within and between states. Accordingly, this pathbreaking Element will attempt to apply insights from evolutionary biology, evolutionary psychology, neuroscience, and archaeogenetics to IR. Among such insights are the evolved role of emotions in decision-making, intergroup competition as a driver of in-group cooperation, and culture, morality, and language as group-binding mechanisms. *Homo sapiens* is a primate, so comparison with the behaviours of other great apes reveals some commonalities in terms of group dynamics, status, and hierarchies, as well as the enduring human capacity for both in-group cooperation and organised violence against other groups. These have an evolutionary basis that is relevant to IR theory and practice.

Keywords: evolution, international relations (IR), complexity theory, human nature, evolutionary psychology

© Jeremy Garlick 2025

ISBNs: 9781009464161 (HB), 9781009464147 (PB), 9781009464154 (OC)
ISSNs: 2752-9428 (online), 2752-941X (print)

Contents

1 Foreword   1

2 Introduction   1

3 The Implications of Evolution for International Relations   9

4 IR's Evidential Deficits: Evolution Enters the Picture   15

5 Applying Evolutionary Science to IR   43

6 Conclusion   65

   References   69

1 Foreword

Writing at the intersection of academic fields with very different traditions – international relations (IR) and the science of evolution – is a difficult task. It is essential to master concepts, theories, and evidence from fields which lie outside the normal remit of one's discipline and to convey why they are important for readers unfamiliar with them. It is also necessary to summarise the main ideas of a substantial tradition in one's own field (in this case, IR). The goal here is to provide a stimulating, pathbreaking foundation for much-needed further research into the connections between evolution and IR rather than to present definitive conclusions.

As far as non-IR scholars are concerned, there is a danger of losing those grounded in empirical work in the natural sciences in the morass of abstract conceptual language typical in the social sciences. I have attempted to avoid this issue by explaining IR theories in as concise and accessible way as possible while attempting to communicate how the science of evolution can introduce important evidence into IR. At the same time, care needs to be taken when introducing evidence from biology into IR and the social sciences in order to avoid possible misunderstandings, misinterpretations, and misuse of research findings. The natural and social sciences do not make easy bedfellows, as the social Darwinism movement of the early twentieth century demonstrates. Accordingly, there is a need to be attentive to nuance and not to oversimplify evolutionary processes in the attempt to apply them to IR.

It is possible that the analysis presented herein will provoke and annoy scholars from both fields. Yet I hope it will also prove useful, if only as the seed of a discussion which urgently needs to begin. As IR scholar Chris Brown (2015, p. 112) puts it: 'Evolutionary biology, and the life sciences in general, are likely to transform the social sciences in the coming decades, and it would be regrettable if the emancipatory potential of this work were to be ignored'.

2 Introduction

Given its relatively concise length, this Element can be no more than a brief introduction to the role of evolution in international relations (IR). Still, since this is a pathbreaking area of research and there are very few publications directly connecting the two fields, there is an urgent need for an exploratory foundation. The simple fact is that with relatively few (and, for the most part, not well-known or much cited) exceptions (Brown, 2013, 2015; Gammon, 2020; Holmes, 2014; Lebow, 2017; McDermott & Davenport, 2017; Rennstich, 2018; Tang, 2013, 2020; Thompson, 2001), IR scholars have paid very little attention to recent research in evolutionary science. Equally, evolutionary scientists, while certainly familiar with developments in global affairs, are probably not abreast with the latest research in IR. This means there is a need to explore the extent to which insights from the two fields, IR and evolution, can be connected; and particularly, how research into evolution can have an impact in IR.

Accordingly, this Element will attempt to apply insights from evolutionary biology, evolutionary psychology, neuroscience, and archaeogenetics to contemporary IR. Among such insights are the evolutionary role of emotions, intra- and intergroup dynamics, and status hierarchies, as well as the evolved function of morality and language as group-binding mechanisms. Understanding these aspects of our evolutionary history and psychology is essential if scholars are to build a firmer scientific and evidential foundation for the study of international phenomena than has hitherto been achieved through the deductive application of IR theories.

As the following sections will outline, there are clearly discernible patterns of behaviour and attitude which derive from our primate past and run into our *Homo sapiens* present. These influence interactions within and between international actors such as nation states. Meanwhile, the academic field of IR remains, seemingly with little awareness, fixed on outmoded assumptions about human rationality which do not match the body of accumulated evidence from evolutionary science and psychology, and which are confused in their application to practical affairs in the real world (Schmidt & Wight, 2023). Conceptual thinking in IR also tends to take place without sufficient reference to empirical evidence from the natural sciences in general, and from evolutionary biology, neuroscience, and evolutionary psychology in particular. In short, IR needs an update based on such evidence rather than continuing to operate without reference to it.

Many scholars of IR tend to assume that politics is the be-all and end-all of what they study. Sometimes it is taken for granted (especially in the US) that IR is merely a subfield of political science (Reiter, 2015). Yet, as this Element will demonstrate there is much more to IR than just the study of politics in isolation. Indeed, what we call politics emerges from evolved human nature, group psychology, and evolved behaviours relating to group behaviours and competition from other groups. Evolutionary psychology, neuroscience, culture–gene co-evolution, language, status, and other aspects of human historical development in fact play a huge – but largely unrecognised – role in relations between states. The set of human behaviours referred to as 'political' emerge from a complex network of factors, many of them with origins deep in humanity's past and in its still-evolving present.

As far as IR theory is concerned, conceptions of human nature were at the centre of classical realism, which was prevalent in IR from the 1940s to the 1960s (Schuett, 2010). A key part of the focus was on supposed human self-interest in the struggle of state against state (Carr, 1939; Morgenthau, 1948; Niebuhr, 1941). In a crude sense, this interpretation tied in to the Darwinian-influenced notion of the 'survival of the fittest', and so there was some connection to evolutionary theory in a rough sense (Knutsen, 1997, p. 197). However, classical realism was critiqued for its lack of a systematic approach to theory-building and reliance on 'unflattering and unsophisticated views of human nature' (Rosenberg, 1990, p. 292). The search was on for a more 'scientific' method to theorisation which could identify causal processes using the language of dependent and independent variables (King et al., 1994). For the most part, IR scholars began to seek explanations of complex international phenomena which employed linear causality and a view (derived from neoclassical economics) of human decision-making as rational. However, this was done without awareness of complex phenomena such as non-linearity and emergence because those had not yet been conceptualised in either the natural or the social sciences. For the same reason, it was also done without reference to recent developments in the study of human evolution and genetics.

With the advent of neorealism after the publication of Kenneth Waltz's seminal work *Theory of International Politics* (Waltz, 1979), the focus of theorising shifted from human nature to the structure of the international system. In an earlier work, Waltz (1959) included individual humans as one of three levels or 'images' of analysis in international politics alongside states and the international system. However, he did not theorise human nature systematically. Waltz claimed that the international system is anarchic, meaning that there is no overarching government to regulate or mitigate individual states' rational self-help behaviour. Thus, competition from states is said to arise from the lack of top-down limitations on their behaviour rather than explicitly from human nature. After this development, human nature as a variable in IR was therefore mostly shelved in theoretical debates in favour of systemic explanations of states' behaviour as driven by competition for resources and survival in conditions of international anarchy. Although Waltz's understanding of states as similar units whose behaviour is driven by competition for resources and power is partially based on a loose interpretation of evolutionary fitness and natural selection (Waltz, 1979, p. 137), it is not based on a rigorous understanding of the science of evolution.

The shift towards systemic explanations based on international anarchy rather than evolved human nature continued even as constructivist interpretations emerged, for instance through Alexander Wendt's (1992) influential article entitled 'Anarchy is what states make of it: the social construction of power politics'. By the 1990s, discussions of human nature had dropped out of IR almost entirely, even in constructivist texts. Nor did they return in subsequent decades, even as the legitimacy of methodological approaches employing linear causal mechanisms was beginning to be questioned by some IR scholars (Garlick, 2020b; Jervis, 1997; Kavalski, 2015). Above all, explicitly drawing connections with biological evolution fell out of favour because of its unfortunate associations with social Darwinism stemming from the abuse of evolutionary theory in the early twentieth century (Brown, 2013, p. 442). At the same time, IR scholars frequently draw on concepts from evolutionary theory such as 'survival of the fittest', often in a metaphorical fashion, while theorising about international politics. However, they generally do this without making the source of the concepts and metaphors explicit and without clearly distinguishing whether they are consciously using terms metaphorically or referring to actual biological processes (Lebow, 2017).

The following sections outline a number of ways in which recent findings from the science of evolution not only *can* be incorporated into IR but also *need to* be incorporated. International relations as a field needs greater input from other fields and more solid empirical evidence to support or contradict scholars' tendency to utilise conceptual thinking in theory-building. Human nature needs to be brought back into IR theories in a way that avoids being drawn into social Darwinism and other unfortunate misuses and abuses of evolutionary theory. This can be achieved by considering empirical evidence (such as that outlined in this Element) from evolutionary psychology, neuroscience, and evolutionary biology.

If relations between groups of humans such as nation states are to be fully explained, it is essential to include phenomena such as culture–gene co-evolution, self-domestication, and the evolutionary basis of intergroup competition and in-group cooperation. For instance, if intergroup competition is an evolutionary driver of in-group cooperation, as claimed by the evolutionary psychologist Jonathan Haidt (2012) and the sociobiologist E. O. Wilson (2012), then this has clear implications for our understanding of ourselves and our behaviour in our own and towards other groups. In evolutionary terms, in-group cooperation is essential if individuals and their offspring are to survive, and may be generated to a great extent by intergroup competition.

Understanding the characteristics of such evolved behaviours can enable us to better harness and channel them for the benefit of both our own group and the whole of humanity. It is imperative to take account of human evolutionary heritage in order to present better normative solutions to international problems such as wars, competition for resources, and climate change. For instance, the evolved tendency to intergroup rivalry and military confrontation may be harnessed and given less harmful outlets by creating more opportunities for non-destructive competition between groups. There are already numerous examples of such outlets, which can be considered a form of conflict substitution. They include international sports tournaments or other contests (for instance in singing or e-sports), in which national representatives are supported by large sections of the public. Another possibility for mitigating the human tendency to instrumental violence between groups is to actively cultivate the evolved trait of self-domestication (which has been a successful survival strategy for humans), encouraging enhanced intergroup cooperation on the principle of 'survival of the friendliest' (Hare & Woods, 2020). Such normative solutions may seem far-fetched or improbable at this point in time; but given the evidence outlined in this Element of ongoing human self-domestication and culture–gene co-evolution, they should not be immediately dismissed as impossible in the long term.

The sections will progress as follows. Section 3 outlines in brief the historical development of the academic field of IR, especially in terms of its thus-far neglected connections to evolution and the reasons why evolution has been left out (primarily because of the appearance of social Darwinism in the early twentieth century). The section introduces several areas of evolutionary research which directly relate to IR. Among these are the evolved role of emotions (rather than what IR generally assumes to be 'rationality') in decision-making, the role of in-group cooperation and competition with other groups as evolutionary mechanisms promoting genetic survival, and the evolved role of status and hierarchy (rather than the neorealist assumption of 'anarchy') as part of the basis of the international order. The section outlines how introducing these factors into the analysis of IR simultaneously challenges and complements existing research in the field.

Section 4 discusses in more detail how evolution can be introduced into specific areas of IR. It examines the main IR theories, specifically (neo-)realism, (neo-)liberalism, and constructivism, identifying areas in which evolutionary science can contribute to or challenge existing theoretical frameworks. Neorealism's focus on rational actors is challenged by work on the evolved role of emotions in decision-making (Damasio, 1994, 2000; Gammon, 2020; Lerner et al., 2015), while its focus on anarchy is undercut by research into the role of hierarchy and status within and between groups (Kang, 2012; Murray, 2019; Storr, 2021). Constructivism's focus on the construction of identity and 'othering' would benefit from examining the evolved role of in-group cooperation and intergroup competition in facilitating the survival of groups, even at the expense of some of the individuals within them (Bowles, 2009). Examining these factors can offer an explanatory basis for constructivism which enriches the use of the theory and gives it a firmer evidential basis in science. Other areas of evolutionary research discussed in this section including and human capacity for both violence and cooperation. This has been much studied in IR, but not in the context of its evolutionary role and explanation of human behaviour and human nature. Similarly, other factors such as the roles of language and morality in IR have been largely ignored by scholars. In general, there have been relatively few efforts to incorporate evolutionary science into IR. Tang's (2013, 2020) social evolution paradigm (SEP), a notable attempt to introduce evolution into IR, sits on the fringe of the discipline and consequently has not yet been given much attention or sufficiently developed. A similar fate has befallen William R. Thompson's (2001) edited volume entitled *Evolutionary Interpretations of World Politics*. More recent attempts to integrate evolution into IR, such as the papers published by Rennstich (2018) and McDermott and Davenport (2017), have not made any significant impact in the field.

Section 5 moves on from IR theory to an examination of how to apply various aspects of evolution to international phenomena. Beginning from an outline of humanity's primate heritage and its implications in terms of evolved behaviour, the focus is on the significance for IR of a range of evolved human attributes. As a member of the primate family, *Homo sapiens* shares a large amount of genetic information with great apes such as gorillas, chimpanzees, and bonobos, making comparative study fruitful in terms of drawing conclusions about human-evolved attributes such as hierarchical organisation, in-group cooperation, and intergroup competition. For example, observation of chimpanzees reveals that they organise into hierarchical bands. These bands manifest both peaceful cooperation within the group and deadly violence against other groups (de Waal, 2005). In humans, Jonathan Haidt's research shows that intergroup competition is a driver of in-group cooperation and that 'the most cohesive groups wipe out and replace the less cohesive ones' (Haidt, 2012, p. 252). This means that intergroup competition is an evolutionary inherited aspect of the human experience, and hence also of relations between groups such as nation states.

Section 5 also examines the impacts on IR of culture–gene co-evolution. This refers to the effects of evolved cultural phenomena such as cooking, reading, or religion in altering specific human genetic characteristics over the long millennia of human evolution. For instance, the advent of cooking produced humans with smaller jaws, stomachs, and intestines than human ancestors or primate relatives such as chimpanzees (Henrich, 2016, p. 65). This type of scientifically demonstrable relationship between cultural shifts and measurable physical (genetic) changes is what is known as *culture–gene co-evolution*.

As far as IR is concerned, some cultural shifts, especially those in Western Europe, resulted in changes which impacted global developments as people from the region spread out across the world during the colonial era. Most notably, the influence of the Catholic church in parts of Western Europe in particular produced a shift over 1,500 years away from kin-based groups to nuclear families, and from villages to adaptation to urban life among a multitude of strangers (Henrich, 2020). As Western Europe urbanised over the centuries, the shift away from large kin-based groups became increasingly prevalent, while general literacy increased, altering cultures, societies, and thinking, especially among elite groups. As people became more individualistic and accoustomed to living among strangers rather than rural kin groups, there was a gradual shift from holistic to analytical thinking. Remarkably, as scientists have demonstrated, this even resulted in some measurable changes to brains such as a thicker corpus callosum between the two hemispheres of the brain (Dehaene, 2009; Dehaene et al., 2010; Henrich, 2020, p. 3).

In essence, cultural evolution away from kin-based ties towards more individualistic relations with strangers in urban settings in elite groups of Western Europeans made them culturally and even slightly genetically distinct (in terms of specific acquired characteristics of the brain due to cultural shifts) from other populations. This had profound impacts on the rest of the world as they spread out across it. Historically, increased analytical thinking gained at a crucial inflection point in history enabled privileged groups of Western Europeans to access specific advantages in relation to other groups such as the development of science and the ability to organise large groups of unrelated strangers into effective military, corporate, and national units. This has important implications for understanding European imperialism, the post-colonial era, and the structure of today's international system, which is based on principles established by Western Europeans such as nation states and geographical boundaries. These systemic attributes do not directly correspond to group organisation and inter-group relations in kin-based tribal societies. However, it is important to point out that differences between Western European elites and other groups are steadily narrowing over time as other regions of the world urbanise, become more literate, and gradually shift away from kin-based family structures to living among strangers. Eventually, as culture–gene co-evolution takes its course among other groups, the Western European co-evolved cultural-genetic advantage, essentially gained because Western Europe elites urbanised earliest, will disappear completely.

Section 5 goes on to examine self-domestication as a factor in IR. Odd as it may seem at first sight, the idea is that humans have, over tens of thousands of years, developed domesticated traits (such as males becoming 'less exaggeratedly male' (Wrangham, 2019, p. 63)). that have enabled them to live in large communities relatively peacefully. Many individuals with criminal or violent tendencies have been removed from the gene pool, making the broad population increasingly capable of relatively peaceful in-group cooperation. The significance of this for IR is to demonstrate the evolved origins of in-group cooperation and the resulting capacity of leaders to mobilise large populations in the service of strategic goals such as territorial expansion through waging war against other groups.

In its final part, Section 5 explores the roles of language, status, hierarchy, norms, morality, and religion in human evolution and IR. Language has a key role in facilitating in-group cooperation and coordination. Often, this is achieved through gossip, which, far from being mere idle talk, is in fact intrinsically linked to questions of status, norms, and morality (Storr, 2021, p. 44; Vince, 2019, p. 119). Researchers have shown that language is a key identifier of who belongs to a group and who is an outsider (Edwards, 2009). Storytelling, religion, and ritual practices are also channelled through language and are tools for building a common group identity. All of these are evolved mechanisms for establishing hierarchies and solidarity within the group; all give the group its unique cultural identity, and enable groups to develop a sense of 'self' and 'other' in relation to other groups (Haidt, 2012). In other words, the group builds up its cultural identity and sense of unity through these evolved mechanisms. Alongside culture–gene co-evolution, groups develop norms and values which distinguish them from other groups, giving the group solidarity as well as potentially enabling them to out-compete rival groups if the group's norms turn out to provide evolutionary advantages (Henrich, 2016). In short, many aspects of evolution impact relations between human groups such as nation states and tribes and therefore demand greater attention within the field of IR.

At the outset, this Element's limitations need to be outlined. Above all, there is insufficient space to cover all the nuances of a wide range of IR theories or the entire science of evolution. Hence, IR theories are outlined in Sections 3 and 4 with broad strokes, bearing in mind that this is sufficient for non-IR readers. A complex eclectic approach is taken, meaning that concepts and theories are deliberately used selectively to frame specific problems under discussion related to evolution in IR, rather than IR more broadly. This is a study of *evolution* in IR, so the focus is purely on aspects of IR theories which connect to that topic. For more detail on specific aspects of IR theories and practice, readers unfamiliar with IR are referred to general introductions such as Goldstein and Pevehouse (2014), Devetak et al. (2012), or Viotti and Kauppi (2001). In more direct connection, the theoretical sections of one of my previous publications (Garlick, 2020b) connect IR theory to the complexity thinking framework used in this Element. Similarly, the science of evolution is covered in as much detail as possible given the limited space, and always in terms of specific aspects which relate to IR.

3 The Implications of Evolution for International Relations

International relations as an academic discipline has a relatively short history of only about 100 years. The field of IR emerged in the wake of the First World War. However, the development of twentieth-century IR – especially realism – was influenced by earlier political or philosophical thinkers. These include Thucydides, Sun Tzu, Niccolo Machiavelli, Thomas Hobbes, and, in IR's liberal school, Immanuel Kant (Devetak, 2012, pp. 6–8; Goldstein & Pevehouse, 2014, p. 47).

The new discipline's initial primary purpose, based on the horrors of 1914–8, was to study the causes of war and to prevent future global conflicts by generating insights into relations between nation states (Knutsen, 1997, p. 203). It was thought that the development of IR as a scholarly discipline could contribute to creating conditions for peace. This continues to be the broad normative thrust of the discipline, even as it has developed numerous subfields: at IR's heart is the goal of understanding and finding ways to prevent or manage conflicts between nations by promoting collective interests, for instance through international institutions such as the United Nations (UN) (Viotti & Kauppi, 2001, p. 64).

In its early decades, an over-optimistic approach called idealism prevailed. Idealism utilised an optimistic view of human nature based on community and cooperation between states (Goldstein & Pevehouse, 2014, p. 47). It claimed, without firm evidence, that a 'harmony of interests' between nations could be established by persuading their representatives to sit around a table and negotiate (Carr, 1939). When this approach, manifested in the League of Nations (precursor of the UN), was seen to have failed after the outbreak of the Second World War, scholars turned to a more pessimistic approach to human nature which soon came to be called realism. Realism was supposedly based on an understanding of human nature which depicted people as selfish and nations as locked together in an anarchic, dog-eat-dog scramble for power (Morgenthau, 1948). Subsequently, during the Cold War, realists advocated managing the presumed anarchy in global affairs through balancing alliances, proxy wars, and nuclear deterrence. Game theory was used to evaluate the interests of actors, whose decision-making was supposed to be based on rational self-help (Snidal, 1985).

From the 1970s to the 1990s, IR underwent a transformation. New, supposedly more systematic theories such as neoliberalism (Keohane & Nye, 1977) and constructivism (Wendt, 1992, 1999) emerged. These attempted to take account of the increasing complexity of the international arena, which now included more and more new actors such as multinational corporations and non-governmental organisations. Yet still, the broad ontological basis for these theories was the unchallenged assumption based on neoclassical economics that human beings – and groups of human beings, such as nation states – were rational actors whose choices were based on calculated self-interest. Important underlying aspects of the most influential theoretical approaches even today – neorealism and constructivism – are thus based on outdated ideas from economics and sociology, which date back to the 1970s and 1980s. The rationalist assumption remains seemingly unaffected by the large body of evidence emerging from the natural sciences over the last half-century concerning human nature, psychology, and evolution. In other words, since the late Cold War period, in seeking to understand the behaviours, attitudes, and motivations which underlie relations between states, IR has largely neglected the story of human evolution as depicted in emerging fields such as evolutionary psychology and neuroscience (Holmes, 2014).

Most notably, neorealism, a highly influential school founded by Kenneth Waltz (1979), is explicitly based on the rational choice theory used in economics in the 1970s. In economics and other social sciences, rational choice has gradually become irrelevant as insights from psychology and neuroscience (for instance, concerning the role of emotions) have been applied (Damasio, 1994, 2000; Herrnstein, 1990). However, the model persists in IR as an underlying premise even amid discussions of the psychological basis of human behaviour. Most notably, Earl Gammon (2020) demonstrates that research in neuroscience on the key role of emotions in decision-making challenges implicit assumptions concerning rationality in IR theory. He shows that 'emotion and cognition form a tight nexus, implicating emotions in nearly all aspects of decision making' (Gammon, 2020, p. 190). Classical realism, which is IR's oldest theoretical framework, with origins in the history and philosophy of ancient Greece, includes some assumptions about human nature (Morgenthau, 1948; Niebuhr, 1941). However, classical realism lacks an empirical foundation based on scientific evidence and has fallen out of favour in the field.

Constructivists discuss the construction of identity in IR but tend to base their analysis on the work of the sociologist Anthony Giddens (1984), whose theory of structuration was developed between the 1970s and 1980s and does not therefore include more recent findings in the natural sciences. In fact, Giddens explicitly rejects the use of evolutionary theory in social and human history on the grounds that 'human history does not have an evolutionary "shape", and positive harm can be done by attempting to compress it into one' (Giddens, 1984, p. 236). He explains further that '[h]uman beings make their history in cognizance of that history, that is, as reflexive beings cognitively appropriating time rather than merely "living" it' (Giddens, 1984, p. 237). However, as Rennstich (2018, p. 18) demonstrates, Giddens' views are based on a misunderstanding of evolution:

> He implies that evolutionary theories leave no room for learning – outside of genetic storage of information – or the role of choice in the adaptation processes. These are widely held misconceptions of evolutionary theory. . . . Learning is, indeed, an important element in evolutionary development.

In the last decade, constructivists have begun to investigate what they call 'securitisation' and 'ontological security', both of which study nation states' perceptions of their place in the international order in terms of constructed security fears. This seems like a good idea in principle; but again, evidentially the research takes no account of recent findings concerning neuroscience and evolutionary psychology, instead relying on non-mainstream psychology studies conducted in the 1960s (e.g., Lacan, 2006). In short, all the main schools of IR theory need updating to include recent findings from evolutionary theory, psychology, and neuroscience.

At this point, it is necessary to point out that applying contemporary research on evolution to IR should be distinguished from the social Darwinist, biological determinist, and eugenics movements which appeared in the early twentieth century. At that time, Darwin's ideas about evolutionary 'fitness' were twisted into a narrative about the 'survival of the fittest' and politicised to support the supposed innate superiority of white Europeans over other races. Misuse of Darwin's work was based on a misunderstanding (or deliberate distortion) of his theory. Genuine scientific research in evolution should be distinguished from social Darwinism and biological determinism, since human genetic heritage is highly complex and intermingled (Krause & Trappe, 2021). Modern humans all belong to the species *Homo sapiens*, meaning that 'everyone on Earth is part of African diversity' (Krause & Trappe, 2021, p. 222). The relatively small genetic differences between human populations are due mainly to groups adapting to novel environments over millennia, sometimes interbreeding (in Europe and Asia) with now-extinct species of humans such as Neanderthals and Denisovans. Krause and Trappe (2021, p. 222) explain:

> Genetic justifications for ethnic conflicts have no scientific basis and should not persist in today's world. It is on the grounds of unscientific claims made during the previous century that the field still has a reputation for smuggling in racist ideologies under the guise of genetic arguments. To the contrary, genetics today is less compatible with race-based thinking than ever before.

Harvard University professor of human evolutionary biology Joseph Henrich (2016, pp. 95–96) expands on this point:

> In the last century, pseudoscientific efforts to formalize folk concepts of race were used to justify much violence, oppression, and even genocide. However, ... our understanding of human genetic variation, derived from studying actual genes, completely dismantles any remaining shreds of the old racial notions. ... The best antidote for pseudoscience is real science.

In other words, a detailed understanding of the complexities of human migration, genetic intermingling, and cultural evolution completely undermines far-right advocacy of 'racial purity'. It is important to recognise that humans, no matter of which race or ethnicity, are genetically similar to each other and share common evolved patterns of thought and behaviour (albeit with variations between groups). This means there is no empirical basis in evolution for social Darwinism or eugenics.

For these reasons, it is necessary to study the evolutionary origins of human psychology and behaviour if one is to obtain a clearer understanding of why complex social groups such as tribes and nation states interact with each other in the way that they do, especially in terms of in-group cooperation and intergroup competition. Here, as the next two sections will reveal, in-group psychology is primarily the product of social and cultural evolution as much as biological evolution, arising from a process termed 'culture–gene co-evolution' (Conning, 2023; Waring & Wood, 2021). Humans have a shared genetic heritage – common physical traits – which has resulted in the evolution of universal abilities such as upright walking, the development of language, sophisticated use of tools, and manipulation of the natural environment. Over time, on the basis of these physical abilities and gradual processes of cultural evolution, including cross-fertilisation between groups, recognisable patterns of cooperative and competitive behaviour appeared which are shared by all humans, but which vary considerably depending on specific groups' cultural norms.

Accordingly, this Element will examine the implications of recent work in evolutionary psychology and neuroscience for IR since, despite the inattention of all but a few IR scholars, some advances in these fields in the last fifty years are pertinent to the study of international politics and relations between complex societies. As a starting point, a few significant examples are presented here, leaving the elaboration of these ideas for Sections 4 and 5.

3.1 The Importance of Evolution for IR

It is sensible to begin with a critique of the still prevalent assumption in IR that the human mind is a rational calculating machine – long since debunked in neuroscience, evolutionary psychology, and even economics. The seminal work of Antonio Damasio (1994) concerning the role of evolved emotions in decision-making and identity formation is an obvious starting point for research into their impact on IR. Damasio shows that the emotional centres of the brain play a key role in decision-making, since individuals with damage to these areas have difficulty making what might be called 'rational' decisions. Extrapolating further, Jonathan H. Turner demonstrates that emotions play a key role in establishing identity within community and intersocietal systems. He shows that, with the assistance of other evolutionary adaptations such as the development of language, emotions enabled humans to cooperate and bond into large, complex societies containing institutions (Turner, 2021, p. 251). His analysis has clear implications for studying the formation of tribes, nation states, and other complex social groupings and their role in international affairs. If evolved emotions are key to decision-making, identity formation, and in-group bonding, then they are also vital for understanding an important aspect of the ways in which decisions are made in national and international politics and how humans relate to other humans, both within and outside their social group (Gammon, 2020).

A second key area, connected to the first one, is the evolved role of cooperation, violence, and morality in the formation of social groups and attitudes and behaviour towards outsiders. Richard Wrangham (2019) demonstrates that humans have evolved the ability to cooperate relatively peacefully within in-groups, but have also inherited a propensity for large-scale organised violence against out-groups. The 'othering' of out-groups and bonding within the community are an evolutionary adaptation to promote the survival of the collective and thence the genes of the individuals within it. Frans de Waal (2005) demonstrates by comparing human behaviour with that of our closest evolutionary relatives – chimpanzees and bonobos – that our capacity for kindness or violence has a basis in our genetic heritage. Disputes within groups are often settled relatively peacefully while conflicts with out-groups sometimes result in extreme outbreaks of violence. Robert Wright (1996) shows that morality is a product of evolved human nature in response to the demands of living in complex social groups, rather than a divine gift or a product of supposedly transcendent rationality. Such findings have implications for understanding why nations wage war with one another while often maintaining relatively peaceful, cohesive relations internally, overcoming intra-group frictions in the service of national unity and collective security.

Another connected area of interest is the role of status and prestige in relations between members of societies as well as between actors on the international stage. There is plenty of evidence to show that status-seeking and hierarchy-building are part of the evolution of human nature. Seeking to raise one's position within a group emerges from the biological imperative of increasing the chances for genetic reproduction (de Waal, 2005, p. 47). It also has the function of creating harmony and stability within the group by establishing a fixed hierarchical order which all members acknowledge, even if those at the bottom of the pecking order may do so without enthusiasm (de Waal, 2005, p. 61). The tendency to measure oneself against one's peers therefore has an evolutionary aspect, as does the tendency to measure one's social group against others. From this evolutionary development emerges the idea of 'us' against 'them' and, in the contemporary era, nationalism (Testot, 2020, p. 29). Will Storr (2021) shows that traits inherited from our primate past drive the human search for status and have an evolved role in complex modern human societies, including the global society of nation states. Michelle Murray (2019) confirms that perceptions of the nation's status and prestige within the international system constitute an emotional driving force of foreign policy decision-making. The role of emotions as nations jostle for status in international society is another factor underestimated by scholars operating within IR's rational choice tradition (Gammon, 2020). The evolved tendency to seek higher status affects IR when leaders and other elites adopt strategies to improve their nation's position in the society of nations today represented by the United Nations. The long-term survival of the group – and the individuals within it – is at stake.

Such insights demand further investigation. Accordingly, this Element will provide a cutting-edge foundation for studying the potential roles of evolution, neuroscience, and biology in IR. A theoretical-methodological approach roughly based in complexity thinking (Kavalski, 2015) will be used to draw eclectically on key concepts from several schools of IR theory (Garlick, 2020b) and connect them to key insights from evolutionary science and neurobiology. The aim is to show, even if this may seem improbable to some readers at this stage, how the science of evolution can be utilised in IR to deepen and enhance analysis of relations between large, complex societies.

If this seems to some readers an ambitious project, well, yes, it is. But it is one worth undertaking in order to expand the boundaries of thinking about IR and to bring scholars of evolution on board. The mainstream in the academic field of IR, while presenting many valuable insights, has in recent decades become rather fossilised in its dependence on distinctions between supposedly incommensurable schools of thought, linear causality, and the rational actor hypothesis. Hence, it needs awakening from what Emilian Kavalski (2015) has called its 'deep Newtonian slumber'. This Element can perhaps be a small prod in the side of the dozing IR beast and at least get it to register that there are possibilities beyond the current bounds of the expressible.

One last point which needs to be noted here is that since this is an interdisciplinary volume, there are likely to be parts of the analysis which are very familiar to one set of scholars or the other, and similarly parts which are likely to represent completely unfamiliar territory for each. The aim is to make the unfamiliar parts accessible to all, while retaining sufficient scholarly rigour and detail to be interesting to those already familiar with those aspects. The IR parts should present something new for IR scholars and yet need to be understandable for evolutionists. Equally, the parts which draw on evolutionary psychology and neuroscience should present something thought-provoking for scholars in those fields while being accessible for IR scholars and other social scientists unfamiliar with the material. Achieving a mix of accessibility and scientific depth is a difficult balancing act, but one to which it is worth aspiring. Above all, this Element is intended to convey the point that cross-cutting ideas outlined deserve everyone's attention and to present the connections between fields with as much clarity as possible.

4 IR's Evidential Deficits: Evolution Enters the Picture

Clearly, IR is a social science rather than a natural science. As such, there are inherent obstacles to conducting reproducible studies. First, there is the complex messiness of ever-changing international phenomena. But most importantly, it is not possible to conduct experiments on nations or other large international actors. Tacitly acknowledging this fact of academic life means that scholars tend to base the foundations of their research on abstract thought rather than empirical evidence. In most cases, conceptual thinking has come to be prioritised, without overt acknowledgement, over observations of data.

Many IR scholars are understandably wary of attempts to bring in hard scientific data as tools for analysing human social phenomena. Data tend to be deployed selectively in support of an argument – for instance, in case studies – rather than as the hard core of the research. Usually, social science research methods examining opinion polls, interviews, speeches, official publications, economic data, or historical analysis tend to be used, and tend to serve the purpose of simply supporting the conceptual frameworks developed at the beginning of the study rather than challenging them. Drawing on the natural sciences does not come naturally to IR, since hardly any scholars in the field are confident about how to work with the data.

Unfortunately, the lack of engagement with the natural sciences is compounded in the cases of evolutionary biology and evolutionary psychology due to those fields' unfortunate historical associations with social Darwinism and Nazism dating back to the late nineteenth and early twentieth centuries

(Paul, 2003). Essentially, in the minds of many social scientists, evolutionary science has come to be associated with proposals for the genetic engineering or eradication of populations considered by fascist and other social engineers of that period to be inferior. Of course, such interpretations of evolution are not only factually erroneous in terms of genetics and evolutionary science, but also morally abhorrent. As such, they categorically have no place in contemporary scientific study. The problem is how to persuade IR scholars and other social scientists that, in the light of the compendious research done in the second half of the twentieth and early twenty-first centuries in the fields of evolutionary biology, evolutionary psychology, and neuroscience, there is an urgent need to bring findings from those fields into analyses of international phenomena, rather than mainly depending on conceptual thinking, theoretical frameworks, case studies, and hermeneutics (interpretation of data). Hence, the focus here is on some of the most influential mainstream and non-mainstream IR theories to reveal areas in which the science of evolution and the development of the human mind have connections to the discipline. However, it needs to be acknowledged that IR theories and concepts can be covered only selectively and briefly rather than exhaustively, given the length of the present Element. Summaries of the key points are placed at the end of each section.

4.1 Neorealism and Neoliberalism

Beyond the use of conceptual theory-building as the cornerstone of the IR discipline, there are other issues impeding the incorporation of evidence from evolutionary science and neuroscience. As a social science, IR is obviously much more closely related to disciplines such as sociology or economics than it is to the natural sciences; and the development of the discipline reflects these roots. Close examination of premises reveals that theories in the mainstream of the discipline such as neorealism, constructivism, and neoliberalism often rest on assumptions derived from developments in other fields in the social sciences. Many of these assumptions date back to the middle of the twentieth century or even earlier. The problem is that while other fields have moved on and replaced earlier theories with ones which take into account more recent research, to a great extent contemporary mainstream IR remains wedded to outmoded theoretical and conceptual frameworks.

A notable example is *neorealism*, which is based on Kenneth Waltz's highly influential *Theory of International Politics* (Waltz, 1979). In this book, Waltz expounded a theoretical framework which still dominates much of Western – and especially US – IR. Waltz's theory is explicitly based on the version of rational choice theory used in neoclassical economics in the second half of the twentieth century. In Waltz's seminal version of neorealism, the assumption is that individuals – defined as *Homo economicus* – base their decisions on rational calculation of self-interest (Havercroft & Prichard, 2017, p. 3; Schmidt & Wight, 2023). The decision-making of the social group – the nation – emerges (via an unexplained mechanism) from the sum of these calculated decisions, situated within an anarchic international environment in which states compete for resources, status, and survival. However one understands it, the assumption of human rationality – whatever that might be – is problematic given recent scientific research into the neuroscience of human decision-making. Despite explicitly including the individual human as one 'image' or 'level of analysis' in his approach to IR (Waltz, 1959), Waltz does not systematically utilise scientific evidence concerning human psychology or evolutionary biology in his theoretical framework, instead focusing primarily on the impact of the 'anarchic' international system on the behaviour of states (Waltz 1979).

As Antonio Damasio (1994) demonstrates, emotions play a key role in guiding decision-making. While conscious thought takes place in the outer layers of the brain, emotions arise from deeper, more ancient areas of the brain such as the hypothalamus. As anyone who has experienced intense fear or excitement will be able to confirm, it is difficult to ignore such emotions in favour of cold rationality, for instance when one is threatened by imminent death. To back up this assertion, it has been demonstrated clinically that some patients with physical damage to the emotional regions of the brain may experience seriously impaired decision-making processes (Damasio, 2000, p. 41). Such individuals may act in ways which are irrational or dangerous to their well-being with complete equanimity regarding the consequences. Essentially, the evolution of the brain and nervous system has created a system which depends on emotional responses to guide rational decision-making in response to cues from the environment or from the individual's internal state. A model which modifies traditional rational choice theory according to more recent research on the role of emotions is therefore needed (Lerner et al., 2015). An additional point is that the decision-making processes of the group (and how they may differ from individual decision-making) are not adequately accounted for – a problem which, as we will see, is a relatively unacknowledged one for IR more broadly.

Thus, basing a theory of group decision-making on the idea that humans are cold, rational, calculating machines capable of ignoring emotions and acting out of individual self-interest lacks a basis in neuroscience and evolutionary psychology, as well as an explanation of how groups reach and enact decisions. In the case of states, there is also plenty of empirical evidence to support the claim that 'states do not always act rationally' (Schmidt & Wight, 2023, p. 179). On the other hand, accepting the empirical and neuroscientific reality does not necessarily undermine Waltz's theory. It simply demands a re-evaluation of the premises upon which it is based, acknowledging that 'rational' decision-making based on 'self-interest' needs qualification or further explanation since the evidence reveals that decision-making – in IR as in other fields – is dependent upon emotional responses to prompts from the external environment and from within the body (Gammon, 2020). In other words, *Homo sapiens* – the biological organism – differs in important ways from the hypothetical *Homo economicus*, not least in having far more complex and context-dependent decision-making processes. The role of evolutionary psychology in consensus building and cooperation in complex social groups also needs to be explained. The next section will probe more deeply into this part of evolutionary science and its implications.

Neoliberal theory in IR contains the same assumption as neorealism concerning human rationality amid anarchy in the international system. What distinguishes neoliberalism from neorealism is the idea that cooperation between nation states and other international actors is possible and desirable. While neorealists claim that conflict is inevitable, neoliberal theorists believe that international institutions such as the United Nations can reduce the incidence of competition and conflict between states (Axelrod & Keohane, 1985). According to neoliberals, processes of democratisation and economic interdependence can produce conditions for peace (Keohane & Nye, 1977). Hence, neoliberals are optimistic about the potential for human groups to overcome differences, while neorealists are resolutely pessimistic, seeing international life as an endless sequence of wars between hegemons and their challengers (Mearsheimer, 2001). In an evolutionary sense, neorealists align with the Darwinian idea that the environment shapes human behaviour, while neoliberals tend in a more Lamarckian direction of humans having agency to shape their response to their environment in a process of 'directed adaptation' (Sterling-Folker, 2001, pp. 89–90).

Interestingly, this polarisation of views between optimistic neoliberals (cooperation is possible and can prevent wars) and pessimistic neorealists (competition and conflict are inevitable) may be capable of resolution with reference to recent findings in evolutionary science. As Richard Wrangham (2019) and Frans de Waal (2005) demonstrate, evolved human nature contains within it the potential for both violence and cooperation, depending on circumstances. Sometimes humans commit horrible crimes such as genocides or bombing campaigns against other groups, but they are also capable of negotiating peace treaties, assisting oppressed allies, and prioritising trade over armed conflict. The potential for cooperation appears to be greatest within the in-group, where it is essential to mitigate internal conflicts for the benefit of the collective in the face of external competition with competing groups (Alexander, 1990). Yet civil wars – internal struggles for power – do occur. Between-group conflicts – wars – have been common in human history, yet alliances between nations also exist. It therefore seems, in view of the evidence, that the polarisation inherent in the neoliberal and neorealist positions is an unwarranted dichotomy. This becomes even clearer when one looks at evidence from evolution and neuroscience.

Frans de Waal (2005) shows that of our two genetically closest ape relatives, one species (chimpanzees, *Pan troglodytes*) is markedly more violent than the other (bonobos, *Pan paniscus*). While humans have not descended from either chimps or bonobos, we do share a common ancestor with them. Both chimps and bonobos belong to the genus *Pan*, from which our ancestors diverged about six or seven million years ago (Krause & Trappe, 2021, p. 35). Where male chimps may resolve intra-group conflicts (especially hierarchical ones) through violence and have been observed deliberately attacking and killing individuals from other groups without provocation, bonobos are more likely to resolve conflicts through peaceful sexual behaviour within the group and do not usually attack other groups as a result of evolved self-domestication towards tolerance and against aggression (Hare et al., 2012). Hence, the evolutionary evidence suggests that the human propensity for both violence and cooperation may be partly genetic and hereditary, and that inter- and intra-group behaviours need to be studied in the light of evolutionary psychology and biology.

In other words, the story of intergroup relations is not as black-or-white as the neoliberal versus neorealist dichotomy presented by IR theory would suggest. Instead, it is necessary to understand interactions between and within human groups as occupying a spectrum of potential from extreme violence to close cooperation. There is also a distinct possibility that competition with other groups has, in evolutionary terms, been the driver of increased in-group cooperation (Heying & Weinstein, 2021). This would imply that competition for resources, status, and survival between social groups has an evolved basis, and that the competitive nature of relations between modern states emerges from evolutionary psychology. Again, the following section will dig into the scientific evidence concerning the relationship between intergroup violence and intra-group cooperation in depth.

As already noted, neither neorealism nor neoliberalism pays much attention to human nature, instead tending to assume a pure rationalism which does not have much to do with reality. An older version of realism – now called classical realism – does base much of its analysis on a pessimistic view of human nature as being rooted in self-interest, competition, and 'will to power' (Morgenthau, 1948; Niebuhr, 1941). What Gregory Moore (2020) has called the 'Niebuhrian' perspective on human nature in IR is informed by a Christian interpretation of the fallibility of human beings as they attempt to navigate between national interests and the role of international institutions in maintaining peace or ending wars. However, the classical realist use of evidence is not systematic and, since it was largely supplanted by neorealism in the 1980s, does not refer to recent evidence from the natural sciences. Again, when critiquing the realist analysis, it is worth taking more account of the inherited human capacity for cooperative as well as conflictual behaviour (see Section 5).

One point upon which most realist and liberal theorists agree is to focus on anarchy as the primary driver of international interactions between states. Anarchy in the sense in which IR scholars use it usually is understood to signify 'the absence of rulers' or 'a system of self-help' (Havercroft & Prichard, 2017, pp. 1–2). However, the assumption that the absence of an overarching world government is the primary driver of behaviour tends to underestimate questions of hierarchy and status in the international system. As in smaller social groups, nation states tend to jostle for position, evaluating their status relationally against others, especially under conditions of male leadership. Observations of apes and comparison with human societies demonstrate that the inclination to build and maintain hierarchies based on status is an evolved tendency with roots in our primate past (Boehm, 1999), even though it is likely to be a relatively mild version containing strong elements of egalitarianism (Christakis, 2019). It may also be a form of social evolution rather than genetic evolution in the strict sense (Turner, 2021, pp. 118–119; Wrangham, 2019, p. 134). Be all this as it may (and more on this in Section 5), in the absence of a world government, competition among states for higher status relative to others is intensified, meaning that what English School theorists have called 'world society' (Bull, 1977; Buzan, 2004) has similar characteristics to other human societies. However, it should be noted that English School theorists also tend to retain the focus on anarchy as the key driver of relations rather than hierarchy or status (Bull, 1977).

An alternative view of the anarchy/hierarchy conundrum in IR is presented by David Kang in a pathbreaking study of East Asian international politics (Kang, 2012). Kang shows that the interstate system that evolved in East Asia was based on hierarchy and status rather than the Westphalian system of supposedly 'like units' which appeared in Europe and the West from the seventeenth century onwards (Waltz, 1979). In Kang's interpretation, relations between nations were based on a tribute system with China as the hegemon (Kang, 2012, p. 11). Kang's hypothesis, which he supports with historical evidence, demonstrates that the assumption of anarchy in the international system may stem from Eurocentric bias due to the predominance of Western scholars in academic IR. This implies that the liberal international order based on supposedly anarchic competition between Westphalian nation states as units is a European invention (and possibly atypical), rather than a universal attribute of intergroup behaviour. Indeed, research done into connections between human nature and cultural evolution suggests that industrialised Western societies are unrepresentative of humanity as a whole, and 'we need to be less cavalier in addressing questions of *human* nature on the basis of data drawn from this particularly thin, and rather unusual, slice of humanity' (Henrich et al., 2010, p. 61; italics in original). It is also worth noting here that historical research in IR demonstrates that notions of territorial statehood and anarchic relations between states may have first appeared in ancient China rather than Europe, albeit with rather different long-term outcomes (Hui, 2005), while aspects of 'European civilisation' such as certain ideas, institutions, and technologies were also appropriated from the East (Hobson, 2004).

As far as IR is concerned, then, scholars are beginning to find evidence of Western bias skewing evidence and conclusions. For instance, a study of China's historical relations with steppe nomads suggests that status-seeking and hierarchical tendencies may turn out to be more characteristic of relations between at least some national groups than anarchy (Kwan, 2016). However, on the whole, reinterpreting interstate relations as situated along a spectrum from anarchic to hierarchic is probably the best course of action. As leading IR scholars Barry Buzan and Amitav Acharya (2022, pp. 119–120) put it:

> Waltz notwithstanding, it may therefore be more useful to think of anarchy and hierarchy not as mutually exclusive categories but rather as part of a continuum, along which all civilizations swing back and forth through history.

Understanding interstate relations in this way also seems to match evidence drawn from evolutionary science and observation of primates (including humans), where hierarchies tend to be mild and leave space for egalitarianism, contestation, negotiated compromise, and cooperation (Boehm, 1999; Christakis, 2019; de Waal, 2005; Turner, 2021; Wrangham, 2019, p. 153).

Key Takeaways

- *The neorealist assumption of decision-making based on rational self-interest is challenged by decades of neuroscientific research on the role of emotions in decision-making.*
- *Evidence from observation of primates shows that humans are evolutionarily capable of both violence and cooperation, depending on circumstances. Both in-group cooperation and intergroup conflict occur. This makes the*

neorealist/neoliberal conflict versus cooperation argument a misleading theoretical dichotomy.
- *The neorealist/neoliberal assumption of anarchy in the international system as a driver of states' behaviour is partially challenged by evolutionary and IR research into the role of hierarchy and status: both anarchy and hierarchy play an important role in human relations within and between groups.*

4.2 Constructivism

Another IR theory which has become increasingly accepted since the 1990s is constructivism. The theory derives from sociology, and in particular Anthony Giddens' concept of structuration (Giddens, 1984). Giddens claims that '[t]he relationship between structures and actors involves intersubjective understanding and meaning' (Jackson & Sorensen, 2006, p. 163). Constructivists also draw on the work of Foucault concerning the relationship between knowledge and power in the formation of social systems (Foucault, 1984). In constructivism, reality is interpreted in terms of ideas and identity construction rather than material factors. This represents a major shift from (neo-)realism and (neo-)liberalism, which focus above all on the material forces which shape interactions between actors and the system in which these take place. For constructivists, '[t]he physical element is there, but it is secondary to the intellectual element which infuses it with meaning, plans it, organizes it and guides it' (Jackson & Sorensen, 2006, p. 165). This implies that ideas 'define the meaning of material power' (Tannewald, 2005, p. 19). For instance, actors evaluate themselves, others, and the relations of power between them through ideational processes of identity construction (Wendt, 1992, 1999).

An example of the application of constructivism in IR is the concept of ontological security. Ontological security is distinguished from the conventional notion of physical security by its focus on identity, stability, and order (Mahant, 2019). Originally applied to the individual in psychology and sociology, IR scholars have extended the concept's usage by applying it to the nation state (Steele, 2007). According to ontological security, states, like individuals, are concerned with stability and continuity. The search for psychological avoidance of uncertainty means that

> [o]ntological security is achieved by routinizing relationships with significant others, and actors therefore become attached to those relationships. … Because even dangerous routines provide ontological security, rational security-seekers could become attached to conflict. (Mitzen, 2006, p. 341)

In other words, the quest for continuity leads to behaviours which may perpetuate patterns of conflict and threat perception instead of attempting to change or resolve them. This leads, counter-productively, to escalating existential risks rather than the pursuit of solutions or change for the better. What appears to be rational behaviour to the actor itself may produce irrational outcomes which include increases in physical threats. The focus on maintaining the status quo and not challenging the existing social order allegedly undercuts attempts at normative transformation and leads to entrenched attitudes and patterns of behaviour.

It is surprising, given the rise to prominence of the concept in IR, that no attempt has been made to link the concept of ontological security to more recent empirical evidence from the fields of evolutionary psychology, neuroscience, and neurobiology. The foundations for the use of concept in IR are, given the state of current knowledge, rather flimsy both empirically and in terms of the extension of the concept from the individual to the state. There is also, as some IR scholars have pointed out, a problem with 'status quo bias' in that the concept theorises only about the tendency to pursue system maintenance and 'investment in the existing social order' (Kinnvall & Mitzen, 2020, p. 240).

Whether it is valid to apply a psychological concept relating to individual perceptions to a social grouping such as a state is one thing. Quite another is the fact that the hard evidential basis for the concept is quite shaky, since its use in IR appears to draw primarily on the theoretical work of the controversial psychiatrists R. D. Laing (1973) and Jacques Lacan (2006), as well as the sociologist Anthony Giddens (1984). This is problematic given that the use of the concept in the IR literature is based largely on the views of two psychiatrists who conducted their research in the mid-twentieth century and a sociologist who explicitly rejected the use of evolutionary science in the social sciences (Rennstich, 2018, p. 18). Their views were formed before the advent of an extensive body of scientific knowledge concerning psychology and neuroscience that is available today. Laing based his use of the concept on a disputed interpretation of schizophrenia as arising from 'a precariously established personal unity' (Laing, 1973, p. 36). Hence, he employed it, as did Lacan, to analyse psychological disorders in individuals. Extrapolating from this to the alleged collective self-identity of large groups of people in nation states is therefore quite a stretch. At any rate, ontological security needs to be seen as existing along a spectrum (Freeston et al., 1994). Some states seek to maintain and preserve their position, but others might seek to improve it. Ontological *in*security – basically, intolerance for uncertainty – is not necessarily equally applicable to all states, but depends on their circumstances and perceptions.

As with neorealism, such problems do not automatically prove that the use of the concept of ontological security is necessarily entirely invalid or incorrect, but rather imply that the concept needs to be tested against the growing body of evidence in the natural sciences; or, if such cannot be found, to be discarded. For instance, it would be useful to know whether human beings cooperating as part of social groups do indeed overwhelmingly pursue status quo relations, or whether they seek to improve their situation by altering the status quo. In fact, as already stated, there is evidence from evolutionary science that increased intra-group cooperation has been driven by intergroup competition (Heying & Weinstein, 2021). Accepting this hypothesis would suggest that evolution has incentivised evolutionarily successful social groups to seek change to the status quo rather than simply to maintain existing relations. It also implies that, in the long-term, groups experiencing ontological security issues and attempting to preserve the status quo rather than developing further would tend to die out. Ultimately, more would need to be done with the ontological security concept in order to distinguish the psychology and attitudes of status quo-seeking groups from those seeking to change conditions in the international environment to their advantage.

Equally, in contradiction of Giddens' distaste for what he saw as evolution's determinism (1984, pp. 236–239), the general theory of constructivism would benefit evidentially and analytically from incorporating research drawn from recent findings in evolution and neuroscience. As far as IR's use of social constructivist theory is concerned, there is a surprising lack of attention to the evolved structure of the brain, the role of emotions, and the role of status and hierarchy in constructing images of other states and social groups. In other words, studying the role of idea and identity construction in IR is a valid enterprise for scholars, but demands to be tied in to the growing body of scientific research concerning the evolution and characteristics of human attitudes and behaviours. Recent research reveals the importance of human agency and ability to shape interactions with the environment. There is also increasing evidence that evolutionary adaptation to environmental pressures capable of being passed on to offspring is possible within the lifetime of an individual (Carey, 2012; Dias & Ressler, 2014). This means that earlier dismissals by Darwinists of Lamarckian interpretations of evolution need to be revised, and the possibility of a degree of human agency in culture–gene co-evolution and other evolutionary processes should be reconsidered (Sterling-Folker, 2006). This appears to be good news as far as constructivism in IR is concerned.

A further example of the possibilities for using findings from evolutionary science in IR pertains to the focus on 'othering' in constructivist theory. Scholars have rightly focused on how identity is constructed and how human collectives tend to divide the world into 'self' and 'other' (Lupovici, 2013; Neumann, 1996). Yet, as with ontological security, the discussion of othering in IR tends to be overwhelmingly abstract and conceptual rather than based in hard evidence concerning evolutionary psychology. Analysis tends to be based primarily on argument, observation, and discourse analysis. This is fine as a starting point but needs further verification, for instance from psychological experiments, field research, or evolutionary psychology. Again, the point is not that the argument is faulty, but rather that it could be made much more convincing by supporting it with observational data concerning attitudes and behaviour towards in-groups and out-groups. Such evidence in fact exists (see the next paragraph and Section 5), but has not been incorporated into constructivist analyses by IR scholars.

Constructivism's analysis of othering may be fruitful in understanding the consequences of the inherited tendency to identify with people who look familiar and behave in the same way as oneself, while regarding as alien or threatening those who look dissimilar, speak different languages, or behave differently. As Frans de Waal (2005, p. 235) puts it:

> Our evolutionary design makes it hard to identify with outsiders. We've been designed to hate our enemies, to ignore the needs of people we barely know, and to distrust anybody who doesn't look like us. Even if within our communities we are largely cooperative, we become almost a different animal in our treatment of strangers.

This behaviour is an evolutionary heritage born of bitter experience. Evolutionary biologist Joseph Henrich's field research in Nepal, Georgia, and Sierra Leone demonstrates that people who have direct experience of warfare demonstrate more solidarity with their in-group than those who have not endured such experiences: conflict survivors adhere more closely to social norms and traditions (Henrich, 2016, p. 207). He goes on to explain:

> During hundreds of thousands of years, intergroup competition spread an immense diversity of social norms that galvanized groups to defend their communities; created risk-sharing networks to deal with environmental shocks like drought, floods, and famines; and fostered the sharing of food, water, and other resources. This meant that, over time, the survival of individuals and their groups increasingly depended on adhering to those group-beneficial social norms, especially when war loomed, famine struck, or droughts persisted. In this world, culture–gene co-evolution may have favoured a psychological response to intergroup competition, including threats that demanded group solidarity for survival. (Henrich, 2016, p. 208)

This analysis demonstrates that there is an evolved rationale for 'othering' which makes sense in terms of the survival of individuals within the protective framework of the in-group in the face of potentially hostile out-groups. Fellow evolutionary biologists Heather Heying and Bret Weinstein (2021, p. 35) expand on this point:

> One clear trend in humans is this: As early humans collaborated ever more with one another to gain control over their environment, their biggest competitors soon became each other. We gained ecological dominance through collaboration, which then set us to focusing on competing with others of our own kind. We cooperate to compete, and our intergroup competition became ever more elaborate, direct, and continuous, until finally becoming nearly ubiquitous in modern times.

It would therefore be an oversight not to take account of the evolutionary role – vital for survival from the prehistoric era up to the present – of cooperation within the group and competition with other groups. Understanding this point can provide rich insight into the inherent obstacles to overcoming othering and self-interest. The assumption in the IR literature on this point seems to be that othering can be overcome if it is consciously understood. It is interpreted – often quite vaguely – as being the result of miseducation, systemic issues, or power structures, as if, should we try hard enough, we can change our inherited mental characteristics. However, a focus on evolution and neuroscience would reveal to scholars a different cause of premeditated violence towards other groups: namely, that there is an inherited basis for such attitudes which is connected to in-group solidarity and cooperation against out-groups (Wrangham, 2019, p. 269).

Constructivism also leans heavily on analysis of discourse to understand identity construction of self and others. Leaders' speeches, interviews, and other official texts are frequently analysed to critically evaluate attitudes. Yet an analysis of the evolution of speech and its role in building group harmony and social cooperation, channelling emotions, forming hierarchies, telling stories, and constructing identity narratives is lacking. So too is an account of how 'othering' through language may be connected to evolutionary psychology as both a group bonding tool and a survival mechanism in the presence of potentially hostile rival groups. This is not surprising when one allows for the fact that constructivism draws on sociology rather than evolutionary science; but still the inattention to hard scientific evidence for eminently sensible interpretations is glaring and demands attention.

At any rate, the use of discourse analysis itself often lacks rigour in the discipline since it is frequently employed unsystematically. Discussions of methodology are often lacking since scholars tend to reject what they see as 'scientism' in mainstream IR (Milliken, 1999, p. 226). The term *discourse analysis* itself suggests at first sight deep linguistic or psycho-linguistic analysis searching for buried meanings in texts. However, many scholars simply refer to the content of utterances or use word maps rather than digging deeper into layers of syntax or semantics, seemingly unaware of this possibility, or perhaps being unwilling to engage with it. Deliberate inattention to scientific methods due to emphasising postmodernism and post-positivism means that discourse analysis, by the admission of its practitioners, 'is not fundamentally about doing rigorous empirical research or developing better theories' (Milliken, 1999, p. 228). Instead, there is a qualitative focus on practices, norm diffusion, power relations, and, in general, how language users construct a version of reality through discourse. Such analysis is not in itself bad in that it points out the agendas underlying discourse emanating from powerful elites; but on the whole it has tended to come at the expense of methodological rigour. There has been insufficient attention to the empirics of language use. As far as IR and evolution are concerned, there has also been a lack of focus on language's key role in promoting in-group cooperation and othering of out-groups in order to increase the chances of the group surviving and prospering in the face of existential threats.

One scholar who has conducted a rigorous linguistics-based analysis in the field of IR is Michael Marks. Across two volumes, Marks (2011, 2018) studies the use of metaphors in IR theory with the aim of revealing the extent to which they are prevalent and constitutive of the central ideas upon which the field is constructed. Marks shows through a detailed exposition of common terms that IR theory, like most human discourse, is based in metaphor, constructing mental images to represent abstractions. International relations metaphors include obvious examples such as the neorealist 'billiard ball' model of interactions between states, but also extend to almost every corner of the discipline (Marks, 2011, p. 6). Marks demonstrates that concepts such as 'structure', 'system', and 'anarchy' are used metaphorically to develop mental images of IR based on physical counterparts in the non-abstract world (Marks, 2011, pp. 30–44). For instance, he notes that the constructivist Alexander Wendt defines anarchy using the metaphor of 'an empty vessel' (Wendt, 1999, p. 249). Marks takes this metaphor to be the basis for Wendt's well-known – but also entirely metaphorical – statement that 'anarchy is what states make of it' (Marks, 2011, p. 31; Wendt, 1992). If one thinks about this statement carefully, the metaphorical (hence not representative of physical reality) nature of a state, conceived metaphorically as an individual actor, making something out of an 'empty vessel' becomes clear. Marks concludes that 'metaphors in international relations theory do far more than simply supply evocative imagery to explanatory frameworks' (Marks, 2011, p. 4). Rather, 'the generally accepted paradigms that are used to analyze international relations are built on metaphorical imagery that provides the very theoretical propositions these paradigms use to hypothesize and make predictions about international affairs' (Marks, 2011, p. 4).

At first sight, the implications of Marks' analysis might be thought to have negative implications for the validity of IR theory. If it is based on metaphor, then can it be said to represent reality in any direct sense? Doesn't the metaphorical nature of theorising in IR and other social sciences invalidate its conclusions? However, this issue is less straightforward than it first appears. Recent research into the evolution of language suggests that the use of metaphor may have had a key role in the transition from more primitive forms of communication to full-fledged human language (Ellison & Reinöhl, 2022). It seems, in essence, that metaphor is what enabled humans to develop linguistic communication in the first place since animal communication lacks any use of metaphor. Metaphor may have been the missing link between protolanguage and full-fledged language. It enabled us to ground abstract ideas in physical imagery, giving them a form which permitted them to be communicated. For instance, every human language uses positionality metaphorically to communicate abstract ideas. We get to the 'bottom' of a problem, we 'arrive at' a conclusion, we 'hide' our feelings (Ellison & Reinöhl, 2022). Such positional language is metaphorical because there is no physical 'place' where they occur. In other words, if metaphor is intrinsic to human language and has allowed us to communicate abstract ideas with each other, then the metaphorical characteristics of IR theorising may be less problematic than they appear.

Nevertheless, there still needs to be a greater acknowledgement by IR scholars of the metaphorical nature of argumentation in the field and its roots in evolution. There are ontological and epistemological implications in terms of the ways in which the human mind interprets and represents reality which cannot easily be ignored. When IR scholars discuss 'soft power' and 'hard power' (Marks, 2011, pp. 96–101), 'spheres of influence' (Marks, 2011, p. 114), 'hawks' and 'doves' (Marks, 2011, pp. 127–129), and the 'Cold War' (Marks, 2011, pp. 115–119), they are using metaphors to represent in words situations and phenomena which exist purely as generated images enabling human cognition and interpretation rather than subsisting anywhere physically on our planet. Ineluctably, such usages tell us as much about our own evolved mental architecture as about the world of human affairs they claim to represent.

In fact, the metaphorical nature of human conceptualisation of the world has been recognised since Lakoff and Johnson's groundbreaking work published in 1980 (Lakoff & Johnson, 1980a, 1980b). They show that the human 'conceptual system, in terms of which we both think and act, is fundamentally metaphorical in nature' and that it 'plays a central role in defining our everyday realities'

(Lakoff & Johnson, 1980a, p. 3). As a key example they elucidate aspects of what they call the 'argument is war' metaphor. They give examples of this in terms of metaphorical expressions such as 'attacking weak points' in an opponent's argument, 'defending' a claim, and landing one's criticisms 'right on target' (Lakoff & Johnson, 1980a, p. 4). As they explain,

> [t]he normal way for us to attack a position is to use the words 'attack a position'. Our conventional ways of talking about arguments presuppose a metaphor we are hardly ever conscious of. The metaphor is not merely in the words we use – it is in our very concept of an argument. (Lakoff & Johnson, 1980a, p. 5)

In other words, our language has evolved in such a way that metaphor is intrinsic to it, enabling us to convey abstract arguments, so that we are unable to speak without it and are not even aware that we are using metaphorical language.

Combining Lakoff and Johnson's analysis with the emerging evidence that metaphor played a key role in the development of full-fledged human language, it becomes clear that there is a pressing need for IR scholars to take a deeper dive into their own and international actors' use of conceptual language. Constructivists in particular need to focus more on the use of metaphor to construct reality, as well as the evolutionary role of metaphor, including in the development of discourse related to and emerging from in-group cooperation and intergroup competition. This would enable a clearer discussion about the characteristics of relations between states through a more objective approach to the subject matter, rather than looking at the material, as many works of IR currently do (either consciously or unconsciously), from the perspective of a specific country or bloc of states. Constructivists point out correctly that we construct our reality through language. Now they need to take this observation further and examine exactly how this occurs and how states construct their relations with each other on the evolved basis of mutually beneficial agreements within the group and constructed images of other groups.

Key Takeaways

- *Constructivist theory's focus on identity construction is valuable but needs more solid empirical support: the theory's basis in psychology and sociology is dated and does not take account of recent research in evolution, neuroscience, and connected fields.*
- *Cutting-edge research in evolutionary psychology can enrich constructivism in the areas of identity construction, othering, in-group cooperation, competition with other groups, and the role of conceptual language and metaphor.*

4.3 Marxist Perspectives

Although they stand outside the mainstream, Marxist or Marxian perspectives are also frequently used in IR theory-building. Most notably, questions of the disparity between the global haves and have nots – often labelled the 'Global North' and 'Global South' – emerge from traditional Marxist discussions of economic inequality and class warfare (Wallerstein, 1974). Marxist theorists thus tend to dominate critiques of the globalised capitalist free-market economic system. Built into this is Wallerstein's division of states into 'core' and 'periphery'. In this analysis, the core states are the ones with the industries, urban centres, wealth, education systems, and so on, while peripheral states are poor agricultural countries which supply resources and labour. Questions of power, hegemony (Gramsci, 1971), and imperialism (Lenin, 1999) are also part of Marxian analyses. Foucault's work on knowledge as power has a partial basis in Marxian thought, as do Frankfurt School critical theory (Held, 1980) and neo-Gramscian research on hegemony, world order and historical change in IR (Bieler & Morton, 2004; Cox, 1981, 1983).

The point to make here is that evidence from humanity's evolutionary past and biological heritage is often omitted from such discussions, or flat out rejected by many Marxists (Brown, 2015). The inbuilt assumption for Marxists and Marxians, similarly as for neorealists and neoliberals, is that humans are – in the long-term, with suitable education – capable of rational decision-making divorced from emotions and our primate past. To an extent, there is a focus on Darwinism in terms of the broad idea of 'survival of the fittest'. However, generally Marxians such as neo-Gramscians base their analysis of global affairs on the interplay of social, political, and economic forces in modern industrial and post-industrial societies without explaining the origins of these forces clearly in terms of human nature (for instance: Cox, 1987).

One of the most important issues emanating from evolutionary psychology and neuroscience for Marxian theorists to address (and which they have not adequately addressed so far) is whether it is feasible to establish a socialist-type system based on egalitarian sharing of resources within the context of large, complex societies. Closely connected to this, and vital for IR, is whether it is possible to introduce a system based on principles of resource sharing and social egalitarianism in the global society of nation states. The main evidence of relatively egalitarian relations within social groups is drawn from anthropological observation of hunter-gatherer societies. However, since these are completely different organisational units with different characteristics than complex modern societies, it is highly unlikely that conclusions drawn from observation of hunter-gatherer groups can be applied to industrial and post-industrial societies. The conditions in which hunter-gatherers prospered have mostly disappeared and they remain in small numbers in only a few parts of the world. The bodies and minds of industrial and post-industrial humans have adapted to modern conditions and are no longer exactly the same as those of our ancestors. We have evolutionarily adapted, both physically and culturally, to conditions in contemporary urbanised or agricultural societies and are not able to return to the conditions of a hunter-gatherer lifestyle even if we wanted to (Krause & Trappe, 2021, pp. 215–216).

A connected point is whether it is possible to avoid establishing hierarchies in large, complex societies with institutional structures, governments, and bureaucracies. Even though liberal democracies have elections in which all eligible adults can participate, this does not mean that power, wealth, and resources are distributed evenly. Countries which attempted to apply Marxist theory to building socialist systems during the twentieth century such as the USSR and the People's Republic of China soon became notoriously hierarchical and top-down in their decision-making and enforcement of norms and rules. The same point applies to institutional arrangements regulating relations between countries, such as the United Nations (UN). The UN has a supposedly egalitarian system of one country, one vote. However, in practice the UN is in fact dominated by the five permanent members of the Security Council. The US, Russia, China, the UK, and France – the victors in the Second World War – have the right to veto any and all measures proposed by the General Assembly. As an example, in April 2024, Russia vetoed a proposal to adopt a resolution calling on countries not to deploy weapons in space (Lederer, 2024). Such demonstrations of veto power reveal an entrenched hierarchy in power and decision-making which can be challenged or changed only with great difficulty, or perhaps not at all. They also provide further evidence of inveterate intergroup competition and the human tendency to mistrust and come into conflict with other groups at the global level.

Thus, it is doubtful that an egalitarian or anarchic system of governance is possible since it is difficult to find historical or contemporary examples of non-hierarchical states, empires, or other large-scale social units. Israeli kibbutzim are sometimes mentioned as presenting evidence of the possibilities of building socialist or anarchist communes. However, they come with a wide range of practical issues relating to human psychology, status, and sharing which have impacted their functioning (Abramitzky, 2018). Even to the extent that kibbutzim have been successful, these are small-scale social groups and not equivalent to nation states containing millions of individuals. This implies that it is important for Marxists (and anarchists) to consider issues of genetic heritage and evolutionary psychology when analysing questions of exploitation versus egalitarianism in nation states, and regarding potential transformations in relations between the Global North and South. If intergroup competition is an evolved survival mechanism, then inequalities and core/periphery gaps may turn out to be inevitable by-products of human psychology and behaviour which can perhaps be mitigated somewhat through international institutions but cannot be reduced to zero. This would mean that the Marxist dream of humans sharing resources equally within and across groups – which was the supposed rationale for the command economy within the Soviet Union and the Warsaw pact countries – is not achievable because it does not adhere to the characteristics of evolved human nature.

Key Takeaways

- *The Marxist focus on egalitarian use of resources seems utopian when considering evidence concerning the evolutionary role of status, hierarchy, and competition.*
- *Marxism fails to account for evolved human nature since, like neorealism and neoliberalism, Marxists tend to assume that humans are rational decision-makers capable of pushing emotions to one side; evolutionary psychology demonstrates that this is not possible.*

4.4 Norms, Ethics, and Normative Issues

Another area of IR theory to which evolutionary science can contribute is normative theory. International relations commonly discusses norms and normative issues, often in terms of human rights, values, and practices. Discussions tend to be complex and wide-ranging, but sometimes lacking in definitional precision and empirical evidence. For instance, analyses of norm diffusion tend to be mainly conceptual, 'fuzzy', and exploratory rather than empirically based and evidentially precise, even when insightfully attempting to address the evolution of norms across time (Winston, 2018). In another example, John Rawls' (1971) seminal work on morality, democracy, and rights, *A Theory of Justice*, is based on a vague conception of human nature without any clear scientific basis, including the assumption that in stable democratic societies human beings are rational decision-makers who will choose to act in accordance with ethical norms (Chapman, 1975).

Across the discussion of normative and ethical issues at large, there appears to be a degree of conceptual confusion between norms defined as practices – behaviour and attitudes that are considered 'normal' by a society – and norms defined as ethical values. On a personal note, when I have attempted to present papers at conferences on China's attempts at norm diffusion in the Global South and Europe (Garlick & Qin, 2023a, 2023b), I have been met with incomprehension and angry responses from some European participants who claim that China does not have any norms. Presumably this is because these participants equate the word 'norm' with a moral, value-based connotation rather than with a practice-based definition. While this interpretation is understandable, it seems self-evident that every nation state and group of human being develops cultural norms and practices to govern in-group interactions, and that intergroup interactions are also often governed by social norms. These may be concerned with behaviour and attitudes which are considered morally correct by the group but can also be simply concerned with rituals or behaviours which promote survival. Quite simply, it is not possible for a social group to exist without norms to govern in-group interactions.

In other words, as with religious questions, it is impossible to evaluate scientifically whether one set of norms is more 'correct' or 'ethical' than another. They are simply different, and the differences undoubtedly influence both in-group and intergroup interactions, as they have done throughout human history. In other words,

> [o]ur social psychology appears designed for navigating a world with social rules and reputations, where learning and complying with these rules is paramount and where different groups possess quite different norms. (Henrich, 2016, p. 316)

Attempting to insist on the universality or ethical correctness of a set of norms is therefore irrelevant to the study of intra- and intergroup interactions over the course of human history in an objective sense. However, the fact that such perceptions exist does in itself provide useful evidence of the role of norms in cultural and psychological evolution within groups.

Thus, whether a specific set of norms is considered ethical or not is a moot point depending on the point of view of the observer rather than anything akin to either a scientific fact or universally accepted value judgement. The Western assumption that evolved Western norms are universal and applicable to all cultures is dependent on the extent to which specific cultures accept or reject those norms, as they are introduced and impact those cultures. While Western norms are steadily being diffused across the rest of the world, this is part of a process of cultural evolution which will likely take centuries, and which has outcomes which are perpetually evolving and transforming in complex processes which are difficult to predict. Such evolutionary processes have no end point or goal since evolution has no end point or goal (Forbes & Krimmel, 2010).

All this means that the study of norms, values, practices, and ethics requires a clear understanding of their evolutionary role as tools facilitating in-group cohesion in the face of intergroup competition. In evolutionary terms, this is their primary function since the survival and ongoing prosperity of the group is their reason for existing. Discussions, mainly by Western-based scholars, of human rights, democracy, and other practices originating in Europe need to take into account the evolutionary role of norms in socialisation, cultural evolution, and group solidarity. For instance, debates about the extent to which the European Union is a 'normative power' (Diez, 2005; Kavalski, 2013; Manners, 2002) need to acknowledge not only the evolutionary role of norms but also the different paths of cultural evolution of social practices in other parts of the world, particularly those which retain kin-based or collectivist ties rather than focusing on the rights of individuals.

Key Takeaways

- *Norms, values, and morality have a basis in evolutionary psychology and in-group cooperation in the face of intergroup competition which is generally not included in IR analyses.*
- *In discussions of human rights and democracy, Western scholars tend to uncritically assume that Western norms and values are universal or automatically acceptable to people in non-Western cultures. In fact, there are major differences in norms and morality across societies, with the West being atypical: this has implications for IR.*

4.5 Complexity Theory

Beyond issues relating to the inattention to scientific evidence in individual schools of IR theory, there is another, deeper-lying problem: the tendency for many scholars to continue reasoning in terms of linear causality using the logic of dependent and independent variables. Since the 1980s, scientists have demonstrated beyond reasonable doubt that reality is messy and that in most cases it is not possible to identify single causes for phenomena (Kauffman, 1995; Prigogine & Stengers, 1985; Waldrop, 1993). This new understanding of complexity and complex systems implies that 'as actions combine to constitute the environment in which the actors are situated and actors in turn change as the environment alters, the language of dependent and independent variables becomes problematic' (Jervis, 1997, p. 58). Complex and non-linear processes underlie many natural phenomena, including the evolved biology and neurology of human beings (Mazzocchi, 2008). Undoubtedly, this is also the case for complex social phenomena such as those which emerge from dynamics within and between nations.

Fortunately, in recent decades scholars have identified some ways to incorporate into IR theory what Emilian Kavalski (2015) calls 'complexity thinking'. Beginning with the seminal work of Robert Jervis (1997), some scholars have begun to introduce ideas drawn from the science of complexity into the study of international politics (Bousquet & Curtis, 2011; Cudworth & Hobden, 2011; Harrison, 2006). Concepts drawn from complex systems analysis such as emergence, non-linearity, feedback, and path dependence seem ideally suited to understanding developments in the international arena due to their capacity for deconstructing processes and changes (Garlick, 2020b, pp. 81–90). The need to frame international phenomena using concepts drawn from complexity theory is especially apposite when considering that future events are often difficult – or impossible – to predict. The occurrence of 'black swans' (Taleb, 2008) or 'grey rhinos' (Wucker, 2016) – events which are uncommon but still inevitably occur at some point and must therefore be prepared for – need to be incorporated into analysis. This is particularly the case in the contemporary era of potentially enormous disruptions to the international order due to the possibility of environmental or natural disasters, global pandemics, nuclear warfare, and so on. As Neta Crawford puts it, world politics is 'an emergent system of multiple interacting systems' (Crawford, 2016, p. 266). Cudworth and Hobden (2011, p. 75) concur, stating that

> [w]hat we call the international is a complex interweave of numerous systems nested, intersected and embedded in each other, all undergoing processes of co-evolution and linked by innumerable feedback loops.

Complexity thinking as an attitudinal approach combined with some insights from complex systems analysis together constitute a suitable overarching analytical framework within which the application of evolutionary science to IR can be situated.

All the same, prominent IR scholars such as Kenneth Waltz have pointed to what they believe to be the need for theoretical frameworks to be relatively parsimonious in order to avoid diffuseness, confusion, and lack of genuine insight (Waltz, 1979, p. 50). Drawing on this principle, Western IR theorists are often keen to distinguish schools of thought from one another, leading to the inbuilt assumption that their analytical frameworks are mutually exclusive or 'incommensurable' (Wight, 1996, p. 319). This insistence on Occam's Razor and analytical incommensurability seemingly leads to a lack of enthusiasm for complexity thinking, or perhaps an inability to fully comprehend it. Put another way, there is a lack of attention among many IR scholars to the fuzziness, non-linearity, and emergent properties of complex systems at the holistic level (Kavalski, 2015).

Regarding the supposed incommensurability of IR theories, scholars have argued that concepts and findings from different theoretical traditions can be productively combined without losing analytical rigour or logic (Garlick, 2020b; Jackson & Nexon, 2009; Wæver, 1996; Wight, 1996). Vital in this regard is the work of Sil and Katzenstein (2010, 2011) concerning what they call 'analytic eclecticism': the use of concepts drawn from a range of IR theories to explain different aspects of phenomena. As Acharya and Buzan (2002, pp. 22–23) point out, 'the realist/liberal/constructivist divide ... is being increasingly challenged within recent theoretical IR literature'. For instance, one might combine constructivism and realism in the analysis of both ideational and material aspects of international phenomena, emphasising the relationship between power politics and social construction in IR (Barkin, 2003, 2010).

In principle, analytic eclecticism might also be used as a broad theoretical-methodological framework for introducing evidence and ideas drawn from evolutionary psychology and neurobiology into IR without creating logical contradictions or incoherence. This ties into complexity thinking, which allows for the analysis of multiple intersecting non-linear phenomena rather than attempting to separate out individual strands of linear causality. The latter may not, in fact, make sense in our complex world based on large-scale societies interacting through multiple channels such as international trade, the internet, industrial production, and so on. Crawford (2016, p. 266) points out that it is only by 'interdisciplinarity, a relaxation of the insistence on parsimony, and openness to the pluralism and complexity of human experience' that we can hope to produce insightful analysis of the messiness inherent in international affairs.

Complexity thinking and complex systems analysis can be brought into the analysis of the intersection of IR and evolution in a number of ways. For instance, path dependence is a key analytical concept for understanding the development of modern, complex societies. New institutions are always built on top of the old ones from which they evolved 'and these older forms are anchored in our evolved primate psychology' (Henrich, 2020, p. 88). Inherited human nature creates path dependence which limits the possibilities for institutional reform, slowing societal transformation.

Emergence is another key concept drawn from complexity theory which has a practical application to human societies and international affairs. Emergence as a term refers to the tendency for self-organising characteristics to appear in complex systems (such as states) which are not self-evident from the qualities of the individual components of the system (such as individual human beings). Phenomena can appear in complex systems that are not predictable based on the appearance of individual parts of the system which interact with each other. The complex interaction of the parts creates new properties in the system (Geyer &

Harrison, 2022, p. 19). For instance, 'a city is an emergent property of thousands or millions of human beings' (Coveney & Highfeld, 1995, p. 330).

Put in simpler terms, emergence refers to the whole being greater than (or different to) the sum of its parts (Jervis, 1997, pp. 12–13). Emergent properties arise from the inherited attitudes within a social system, forming institutions, attitudes, and behaviours which promote the interests and survival of the group, but without any of the members necessarily being conscious of the reasons why these specific characteristics are successful. The emergent characteristics of a human group may appear because of pressures created by intergroup competition, producing greater in-group cooperation and driving cultural adaptations (even without conscious decision-making) which enable the group to prosper and out-compete other groups (Haidt, 2012).

In Western societies, such cultural adaptations include living in nuclear families amidst strangers rather than in traditional kin-based groups, adopting notions of individual rights and universal laws, creating impersonal market economies and voluntary associations, and many other related phenomena (Henrich, 2020, pp. 473–474). In Western Europe, these developments arose over centuries from the complex emergent properties of an evolving social system rather than any specific conscious decision-making by individuals. From this base, Western European elites enriched themselves, forged modern industrialised states with new systems of governance, and outcompeted kin-based systems in other parts of the world. The impact of Western European activity across the world radically altered the characteristics of international affairs, as Europeans forced their norms, whether consciously or unconsciously, upon other societies, pressuring them to change in order to survive.

Many non-Western societies have subsequently transformed in some areas (such as adopting market economies or Western systems of governance). However, the degree to which they have adopted, adapted, or rejected Western norms has varied due to path dependence in areas such as the residual strength of kin-based ties. For instance, this can account for the US difficulties with introducing Western-style democracy in Afghanistan. When elections were held, rural Afghanis preferred to vote for candidates within their kin groups, preserving rather than changing the existing patterns of relations and social order (Ansary, 2010, p. 352). While Europeans and their descendants became conditioned over the centuries to place trust in strangers, people in other cultures continued to rely on kin-based relations: the Afghanistan case reveals that this appears to be something that cannot be changed within a mere few years.

Historical, cultural, and societal developments such as these provide evidence of the impact of emergent properties and path dependence in complex social systems on the course of international affairs. Section 5 will expand further on these and other complex phenomena such as culture–gene co-evolution, the impacts of intergroup competition on in-group cooperation, and self-domestication as an evolutionary result of the complexification and urbanisation of societies, presenting many new avenues for research on the intersection of complexity, evolution, and IR.

Key Takeaways

- *Initernational relations theory needs to incorporate complexity thinking rather than depending on linear causality: human societies are complex adaptive systems within which evolution contributes to historical development and ongoing complexification.*
- *Complexity theory provides concepts such as emergence and path dependence which connect evolution with IR via culture. For instance, complex modern societies have emergent properties and path dependencies, such as contemporary European social organisation around urban centres and nuclear families, which are products of cultural evolution.*

4.6 Tang's Social Evolution Paradigm

Within the field of academic IR, the foremost systematic attempt to bring evolutionary science to bear on the problems of IR specifically is Tang Shiping's SEP. He applies SEP to IR in his volume entitled *The Social Evolution of International Politics* (Tang, 2013). A second book, entitled *On Social Evolution: Phenomenon and Paradigm* (Tang, 2020), covers social evolution more broadly, with reference to Darwinian and Lamarckian versions of natural and artificial selection.

In his 2013 book, Tang suggests that human societies are systems subject to evolutionary pressures and that the international system can be characterised as an evolving society of steadily complexifying human groups which are increasing in size but reducing in number. He claims that the international political system has transformed over the last 10,000 years from an 'offensive realism world to a defensive realism world; and from the defensive realism world to a more rule-based world' (Tang, 2013, p. 5). By this he means that the aggressive empire-building characteristic of previous eras of human history has given way to a nation state era in which territories are fixed. States seek to defend themselves rather than attempting to expand, since the potential downsides of attacking other states have become too high. The introduction of international institutions such as the United Nations and the World Trade Organisation has caused another shift in the direction of rules-based governance of relations between states.

According to Tang (2013), the process by which states and interstate warfare emerged historically is as follows. As human populations increased and turned to agriculture, groups interacted with each other more often amid greater competition for resources. As a consequence, wars became more frequent and larger in scale. Human groups had to fight for survival, and smaller bands and tribes allied together to create larger proto-states. At the same time, military technologies improved, allowing for more efficient means of inflicting violence. The agricultural revolution was also in progress as larger-sized human groups shifted away from hunter-gathering, meaning that groups had to protect their arable land from invaders. All of this meant that state-type units emerged, with ever-increasing capacities to mobilise and maintain armies. Often, it made sense to try to eliminate rival groups and annexe their territory in order to promote the interests and prosperity of the growing state. As states grew in size and eliminated or absorbed other groups, the number of states steadily declined and the ones that survived were larger. This is a point supported by Jared Diamond's research in his magisterial book *Guns, Germs, and Steel* (1997), in which he states that

> [o]ver the past 13,000 years the predominant trend in human society has been the replacement of smaller, less complex units by larger, more complex ones. ... More complex units don't always conquer less complex ones but may succumb to them, as when the Roman and Chinese Empires were overrun by 'barbarian' and Mongol chiefdoms, respectively. But the long-term trend has still been towards large, complex societies, culminating in states. (Diamond, 1997, p. 281)

Eventually, Tang points out, this process of consolidation into larger state-like units meant that it became increasingly difficult to conquer other groups, forcing states to replace offensive, empire-building strategies with a more defensive approach protecting gains already made (Tang, 2020, p. 174). In the contemporary (nuclear) era, for the most part, nations have realised that the risks inherent in all-out attack are too great and it makes more sense to defend what one already possesses. Military technology has advanced to a point (for instance, nuclear weapons) where it can be insanely risky to attack other states. Institutions such as the UN and the WTO have emerged to establish some rules to govern international affairs. Even if these institutional arrangements are not always respected by all actors, the mere fact that they exist is a shift from the anarchy of previous eras in which there were no such institutions. This is why Tang hypothesises an evolution from an 'offensive realism world' to a 'defensive realism world', and a current transition to a 'rule-based world' based on neoliberal principles (Tang, 2013).

Tang's analysis is pathbreaking for IR in its interpretation of the long course of human history and the evolution of intergroup competition. On the other hand, although Tang's social evolutionary framework for analysing the transformation of international politics accounts for historical change to the system, unlike other IR theories such as neorealism (which includes states as units but does not consider their evolution from smaller units or their possible transition into other units) and has solid internal logic, there are some aspects of system dynamics that are not fully worked out. For instance, in his 2013 book Tang posits that ideas constitute the 'genes' of social evolution, while institutions and culture are the 'phenotypes' (Tang, 2013: 27). However, it is not entirely clear whether this depiction is to be understood metaphorically or literally; the implications of these ideas are never fully explained, not even in the second book (Tang, 2020). As Dietl (2008) points out, it is essential for Darwinian theory of natural selection to identify the units involved in evolutionary processes of change. Principles of variation, selection, and inheritance require individual units and specified mechanisms enacting change, be these genes, phenotypes, biological organisms, complex societies, or something else. Uncertainty regarding the causal processes of evolution in IR means that the use of evolutionary theory in IR is still at only an embryonic stage. As Dietl puts it, '[m]oving beyond conceptual frameworks ... seems a necessary step forward' since 'like organisms in nature, entities in international relations are more than just hypotheses of their environment; they also create their surroundings' (Dietl, 2008, p. 98).

Tang also does not devote much attention to questions of evolved human nature (de Waal, 2005; Turner, 2021; Wrangham, 2019) or culture–gene coevolution (Corning, 2023; Waring & Wood, 2021). This is because he appears to believe that it is not productive to consider questions about human nature since 'it is only part of the story of social evolution at best, and our obsession with human nature reflects our impulse of reductionism and thus is conceptual misinformation at worst' (Tang, 2020, p. 112). He also explicitly declines to discuss 'prominent phenomena' such as language, mind, cognition, culture, political hierarchy, and 'key human traits' such as cooperation, morality, altruism, and selfishness (Tang, 2020, p. 5). His reasoning, oddly, is that 'they are only key components, not the whole, of social evolution' (Tang, 2020, p. 5). He goes on to explain further that

> they cannot be adequately understood unless being put into the overall context of social evolution. As such, starting with some specific phenomena or traits in social evolution may be unnecessary for a broader picture-like understanding of social evolution.

As a result of his deliberate choice not to consider questions of evolved human nature, Tang does not wholly manage to bridge the research gap between evolutionary science and IR. As already stated, Tang's first work (Tang, 2013) focuses mainly on IR problems such as warfare, the characteristics of states, and interstate competition. The follow-up volume (Tang, 2020) emphasises the relationship between evolutionary theory and the SEP at a rather theoretical level, but without making much clearer the precise mechanisms of how evolution acts upon international phenomena. Tang's SEP utilises a macro-level interpretation of international affairs in human history which synthesises and solves problems arising from the apparent contradictions inherent in the IR theories of offensive realism, defensive realism, and neoliberalism. However, he does this without incorporating the empirics of recent findings in evolutionary psychology and biology. This means that the SEP remains mainly a broad framework for analysis, rich in Darwinian and Lamarckian theory about natural selection but intentionally short on specifics about processes and mechanisms of cultural and biological change in individuals and groups. As a result, Tang's analysis of the evolution of interstate interactions and warfare is solid but surely needs to be connected to recent work on the intersection of evolution in human nature and culture. This includes research by scholars such as Turner (2021), Wrangham (2019), Henrich (2010, 2016, 2020), Testot (2020), Wright (1996), de Waal (2005), Krause and Trappe (2021), Heying and Weinstein (2021), and many others concerning the evolution and intersection of human psychology, biology, and culture.

Rather than follow Tang's mainly deductive approach based on a primarily theoretical discussion of the role of Darwinian evolution in social affairs, it may be more profitable to identify specific empirical evidence as an inductive foundation for further theory-building. There are numerous insights in the literature on evolutionary psychology, evolutionary biology, and anthropology that can be used, some of which have already been mentioned in this section, but which for the most part have not been included in Tang's SEP framework. These insights, based on scientific findings from peer-reviewed anthropological and primatological research, psychological experiments, palaeontology, and neurobiological data, will be considered in greater depth in Section 5. Such insights include the following: the role of status and hierarchy both within and between groups (Storr, 2021); the role of language and gossip in reputation and status-building (Wrangham, 2019, p. 135; Wright, 1996, pp. 220–221); self-domestication as an enhancer of more intense in-group cooperation (Wrangham, 2019); intergroup competition as a driver of greater in-group cooperation (Haidt, 2012); the role of morality as a tool for in-group cohesion (Wright, 1996); the role of emotions in decision-making (Damasio, 1994, 2000; Gammon, 2020; Lerner et al., 2015); the impacts (including on international affairs) of European culture–gene co-evolution away from kin-based psychology (Henrich, 2020; Henrich et al., 2010); genetic adaptations co-evolving with increased in-group socialisation and cooperation during mankind's evolutionary history (Conning, 2023; Waring & Wood, 2021); and the emergence of hierarchical societies (Testot, 2020, p. 48).

Key Takeaways

- *Tang Shiping's SEP is the only attempt so far to analyse IR through the lens of evolution.*
- *However, Tang's theory is based on a mainly deductive approach which extrapolates from Darwinian theory of natural selection rather than focusing on empirical evidence.*
- *Thus, there is a need for an inductive approach connecting evolution with IR which explores the role of language, emotions, status, norms, morality, self-domestication, and other phenomena. This Element makes a start with this task.*

This section has analysed the implications of evolutionary science for IR in terms of areas in which there appear to be direct connections to existing IR theories. The analysis was framed in terms of the IR theories themselves, identifying points at which evolutionary science intersects with academic IR. Many fruitful areas for research have been identified, including the role of emotions versus rationality, intergroup competition versus in-group cooperation, and the roles of identity construction, status, and language.

The next section will move on to a more detailed and in-depth examination of evidence relevant to IR from evolutionary biology, evolutionary psychology, and other related fields. The aim is to explore some of the research findings that have emerged in the past several decades prior to the publication of this Element which can inform debates within and about IR between nations and other actors. As the section will reveal, there is a wealth of evolution-based research being conducted into the relations between and within groups that are relevant to IR. However, such research is generally being conducted outside the field of academic IR (with the notable exception of Tang, 2013, 2020). The aim of the analysis is to point out the aspects of evolutionary research which are relevant to IR so as to reveal productive avenues for future research into the impacts of evolved human nature in IR.

5 Applying Evolutionary Science to IR

The focus of this section is on inductively drawing out specific findings from evolutionary science which have implications for the study of international relations in general, and for the academic field of IR in particular. Thus, the focus will move away from IR theory to areas of scientific work on human evolution which directly intersect with phenomena studied in academic IR, but which are not generally discussed in this form by IR scholars. Aspects of IR which scholars of evolution have addressed (generally without mentioning academic IR or political science except in passing) include intergroup competition and in-group solidarity, the role of status and hierarchy in relations between and within groups (Storr, 2021, Testot, 2020, Turner, 2021), discussions of human beings as rational or emotional actors (Gammon, 2020; Lerner et al., 2015), and the role of morality and religion as facilitators of in-group cohesion (Henrich, 2016, 2020).

Again, the reader is reminded that the discussion is drawn from a wide range of sources and based on hard evidence in the natural sciences concerning the evolution of human nature, the brain, the role of emotions in decision-making, and so on. The scholars referenced in this section are experts in evolutionary psychology, evolutionary biology, anthropology, neuroscience, and other related fields. Their findings are based on these and other scholars' many years of scientific observation and experimental evidence. They have nothing to do with social Darwinism or other unscientific speculation which has tended to taint the reputation of evolutionary science in the eyes of social scientists. As such, their work is vitally important for building an inductive, evidence-based foundation for research into interactions between and within large groups of human beings such as modern nation states. It would be unwise to ignore it. Doing so would only impoverish science and IR.

5.1 Humanity's Primate Heritage

Many of the scholars whose work is referenced in this section utilise observations from the behaviour of great apes: gorillas, chimpanzees, bonobos, and orangutans. It is important to note that this is *not* because we are descended from these apes (we are not), but because we *share a common ancestor* which lived millions of years ago. We belong to the primate strand of evolution, which means that there are biological traits which are common to all great apes, including *Homo sapiens*. Laboratory analysis has revealed that we share a large proportion of our genetic material with chimpanzees, although researchers are still trying to establish the precise degree of similarity (Suntsova & Buzdin, 2020). Our evolutionary path is thought to have diverged from our closest living biological relatives – chimpanzees and bonobos – approximately six million years ago, and from gorillas around nine million years ago (Testot, 2020, p. 6).

The comparison with apes is useful from the perspective of studying human evolution in terms of traits shared with apes, as well as traits which are unique to humans. The opportunity to compare genetic heritage, behaviour, and biological traits is especially important since all other species of hominids (such as Neanderthals and Denisovans) are extinct, presumably due to being eradicated by *Homo sapiens*, whether by design or by accident (Longrich, 2019). This leaves anatomically modern humans as the sole survivor in the line of evolution which diverged from other apes, although researchers have found that some humans carry Neanderthal and Denisovan DNA, proof of some intermingling between the species (Krause & Trappe, 2021, pp. 36–37).

The importance of understanding inherited traits which are similar in *Homo sapiens* and its nearest surviving relatives (chimps and bonobos) seems to have been lost on some social scientists, including some IR scholars. As outlined in previous sections, there seems to be a tendency to cling to an outmoded presumption of the uniqueness and supposed 'rationality' of human beings compared to presumably 'irrational' animals. Although, of course, humans have developed a wide range of abilities which far exceed those of other animals, this does not mean that we have somehow completely overcome the biological heritage of our pre-human past. The human brain has areas which allow for conscious reasoning and which apes do not have, but also areas which we share with our closest relatives, and areas which we share with many other animals. Our 'rational', conscious minds are built upon parts of the brain and nervous system which operate without our conscious input and govern important aspects of our behaviour. For instance, it has been demonstrated that the amygdala and the remainder of the limbic system are the seat of primary emotions such as fear, and that these are wired into us as crucial reactions to certain stimuli such as localised imminent danger of death (Damasio, 1994, pp. 131–134). Individuals with damage to these and other vital areas of the brain may experience impaired decision-making, even though they may have no diminishment of intellectual capacity (Facundo et al., 2002). This means that the role of emotions and the body as decision-making signalling systems and the basis of consciousness should not be underestimated. Equally, the role of consciousness in decision-making should not be overestimated, since the brain areas responsible constitute only one part of the central nervous system. This functions as a complex system with many moving parts, of which unconscious inputs to decision-making constitute an important aspect (van Gaal et al., 2012).

As an example of what can be learned from the comparison of humans with their ape relatives, Jonathan Turner (2021, p. xviii) points out that apes are more individualistic, more mobile, and far less social than monkeys. This is due to the relative scarcity of food in the jungle environments in which apes evolved and in which they still live today, which means that apes are forced to minimise time spent in close proximity to one another as they roam in search of resources (Testot, 2020, p. 12). As far as humans are concerned, this biological reality leaves us with a genetic heritage of relative individualism that we share with other great apes. Great apes such as chimpanzees tend to have weaker social ties than monkeys and to form relatively small family groups in which individuals often spend time alone (Turner, 2021, p. 33). Our inherited tendency to individualism necessitated the evolution of traits such as proto-language among our hominid ancestors which enabled closer social bonding, coordination, and cooperation in order to survive in the very different environments into which relatively small groups of ancestors migrated (Turner, 2021, p. xviii). Thus, humans have been forced by circumstances to become more sociable than their genes dictate, and in the process have evolved the ability to weave complex webs of social ties which are beyond the capacity of other apes. For instance, chimpanzees standardly live in groups of forty to forty-five individuals, but modern humans live in cities containing millions of inhabitants (David-Barrett, 2023). As biological anthropologist Richard Wrangham (2019, p. 8) puts it:

> Human societies consist of families within groups that are part of larger communities, an arrangement that is characteristic of our species and distinctive from other species.

Since chimpanzees and bonobos are our closest relatives, there has been much discussion of the extent of our similarity to them. Wrangham makes a case that the human capacity for both premeditated violence and altruism is shared with our great ape cousins. In support of this idea he cites the propensity for male chimps to deliberately seek out and kill males from rival bands of chimps as evidence of an inherited capacity for premeditated violence against members of other groups (Wrangham, 2019). At the same time, the apparent tendency of bonobos – among whom females tend to play a more dominant role (de Waal, 2005, p. 63) – to solve disputes through sex rather than violence has been noted as a sign of our evolved ability to make love not war when it suits us.

Thus, humans seem to have a chimp-like tendency for violence and a bonobo-like tendency for cooperation (Wrangham, 2019, p. 9). However, of course, these tendencies exist along a spectrum since obviously both chimps and bonobos are capable of violence and cooperation. Be this as it may, it is clear that humans have evolved the capacity for both great cruelty and kindness, generally (but not always) reserving the former for those outside the in-group who may threaten (or at least not promote) survival, while saving the latter for close kin and in-group members. There is an inherent logic to this observation which goes beyond the much-discussed distinction between chimps and bonobos, but certainly has an evolutionary basis in the need to boost the interests of the group at the expense of competing groups.

Another factor that distinguishes humans from other animals is the ability to manipulate the environment. It is the development of culture that has allowed humanity to escape the constraints of natural selection by changing surroundings to which we are not naturally adapted (Testot, 2020, p. 9). As a result, humans transitioned into an era of culture–gene co-evolution, in which they created tools, walked upright, developed larger brains, increased the range of their diet, socialised, and began to use language. They became 'omnivorous, imaginative, and cooperative' (Testot, 2020, p. 28), and even collectivised child rearing (Testot, 2020, p. 29). It is this transition from natural selection into culture–gene co-evolution that constitutes the major distinction between us and our primate cousins. It also forms the basis of our ability to form larger and more complex social groups which interact with each other, producing – by a process of emergence over many millennia – what we now call relations between nations.

Key Takeaways

- *Comparing humans and apes can be productive: for instance, like humans, apes are capable of both close in-group cooperation and coordinated violence against other groups. This suggests a genetic and evolutionary source of these behaviours.*
- *Like us, apes are relatively individualistic (compared to monkeys). To transcend our individualistic genes in order to survive in groups, we have evolved traits such as language which enhance social bonding.*

5.2 Culture–Gene Co-evolution

Evolution has long been theorised in terms of Darwinian natural selection and Mendelian genetics. In the classical version of evolutionary theory, biological shifts through generations emerge from the so-called survival of the fittest. This phrase represents the idea that individuals with genes which are better suited to local conditions tend to outlive and out-reproduce those with genes that are less well-suited. For instance, genes giving resistance to a specific disease prevalent in the environment produce better chances of survival. Random mutations also occur, some of which produce adaptations which assist with survival. Such genes, perhaps belonging to a small minority, then become more widespread in the population over time, since individuals with those genes pass them on while individuals without them (or with mutations that cause illnesses) mostly die. Over time, individuals with genes better adapted to environmental conditions become more numerous in the surviving population. Through this process, in the surviving population the once-rare variation becomes more common. For instance, in humans, sweat glands and hairlessness likely appeared in this way, since they allowed individuals with those mutations to run further and hunt better than those without them, who were therefore unable to compete and died out (Krause & Trappe, 2021, pp. 11–13).

However, there is now increasing evidence that the standard explanation of natural selection and genetics, while still undoubtedly valid, does not account for the whole story of human evolution. As humans have developed greater mental abilities, and societies have become more complex, culture has begun to play a role in evolution. Humans have evolved the ability to learn and transmit valuable cultural knowledge which increases the chances of individual and group survival. Cultures also evolve to adapt to changing circumstances and to compete with other societies. This has especially been the case over the past few hundred thousand years, as humans have formed larger and larger social groups. As societies have grown ever more complex and individual roles within them more numerous, cultures have evolved at an increased pace. In the past 10,000 years, with the advent of agriculture, advances in science and technology have also impacted cultural evolution, even more so since the industrial revolution (Henrich, 2016, p. 323).

There is a growing body of evidence that cultural shifts have driven genetic evolution in humans in a process of culture–gene co-evolution which directly links some aspects of genetic evolution to cultural adaptations (Chudek & Henrich, 2011; Waring & Wood, 2021). Researchers believe that in the course of human evolution, cultural shifts produced specific genetic changes, for instance increasing brain size to accommodate increasing amounts of cultural information needed to ensure the survival of the group (Muthukrishna et al., 2018). Sociologist Jonathan H. Turner agrees that

> [h]uman emotion, thought, action, and organization thus began to be driven as much by cultural as genetic codes. And, once articulated speech, expanded subcortical and neocortical portions of the brain, and culture existed among late hominins and early humans, they would operate to *intensify all other preadaptations and behavioral propensities*. (Turner, 2021, p. 126, italics in original)

A specific example of culture–gene co-evolution is the advent of fire and cooking, a culture shift which produced smaller teeth, less powerful jaws, short colons, and reduced ability to deal with plant toxins (Testot, 2020, p. 33; Wrangham, 2009). Another more recent example is the spread of literacy in industrialising European societies in the last millennium, which led to changes in the brain, altering the brain areas which deal with language and facial recognition (Dehaene, 2009; Henrich, 2020, pp. 3–4).

In its evolutionary sense, then, culture includes more than just art, music, and literature. The word refers to all forms of knowledge that enable the group to prosper. For instance, it can include know-how such as the crafting of objects such as weapons or boats, the preparation of food to make it edible (Testot, 2020, p. 32), and the performance of rituals which bind the group together. Group contact and solidarity means that culture varies from group to group in important ways. While humans are genetically similar, culture varies to a much greater extent than may at first sight be apparent. For this reason, culture is what distinguishes one group from another. At the same time, culture is only 'superior' in the sense that it may give one group advantages over another in terms of the enhanced ability to survive and prosper in a specific environment or context.

It is important to understand that the evolution of culture, just like that of genes, has no end point and therefore should not be understood as either superior or inferior to what came before except in terms of adaptation to ever-altering conditions. Rather, cultural knowledge is continuously changing as new generations replace old ones and societies become more complex, with more roles and forms of knowledge developing while others disappear (Henrich, 2016, pp. 323–326). Genetic evolution occurs more slowly than cultural evolution because it involves biological changes, and these tend to occur gradually through generations, while group-level cultural adaptation can occur more rapidly by altering the behaviour of individuals within one, two, or a few generations (Waring & Wood, 2021). At the same time, it has been demonstrated that it is possible for epigenetic changes to DNA to be passed down from one generation to the next, for instance in reaction to extreme danger or trauma (Carey, 2012). Researchers have found that responses to traumatic experiences in parents are passed on to offspring through altered DNA in sperm, meaning that inherited behaviours can be transmitted in just one generation (Dias & Ressler, 2014). Through these and other mechanisms such as self-domestication (see next section), human societies are constantly evolving both culturally and genetically, with changes appearing through the interaction of social and biological processes.

As far as IR is concerned, culture–gene co-evolution has caused an important transformation in what we now call the West, defined broadly as the contemporary societies which emerged in Western Europe and countries which were populated by some of them, such as the US and Australia. This evolutionary shift, which took place over the last 1,500 years, is one which has not yet been acknowledged in IR. This is because it comes from the recent work of the evolutionary biologist and anthropologist Joseph Henrich and his research associates concerning some co-evolved differences between Western and non-Western cultures. Henrich posits that there are measurable culture–gene co-evolved differences between people from WEIRD (Western, Educated, Industrialised, Rich, Democratic) societies and those from more traditional kin-based cultures (which were historically prevalent but are now reducing in number as more and more people shift to urban environments and gain access to modern education). Broadly speaking, WEIRD is a shorthand for those societies which industrialised and urbanised first, namely regions of Western Europe and North America, as well as other countries which were populated by Western Europeans. Even though the acronym to an extent occludes the wide range of characteristics possessed by peoples both within and outside Europe, Henrich demonstrates that there are some important co-evolved cultural-genetic differences between WEIRD societies and traditional kin-based societies, with reference to a wide range of psychological, anthropological, and neurological data (Henrich et al., 2010, 2020).

Historically, in parts of what is now considered Western Europe, according to Henrich's research, there was a shift from holistic to analytical thinking which emerged, in large part, due to the switch over many centuries from kin-based ties in close-knit rural communities to societies based on nuclear families and living in large urban centres among strangers. This social transformation was caused, at least in part, by a combination of the influence of the Catholic church in banning marriages between relatives in order to prevent wealth remaining in family groups (Henrich, 2020, p. 161); and, later, the influence of the Protestant church in encouraging worshippers to read the Bible for themselves (Henrich, 2020, pp. 9–13). The result was an increase in individualism, entrepreneurship, and intergroup competition; but it also caused a change in people's thinking, including physical changes in the brain. Such changes included a thickening of the corpus callosum, 'which is the information highway that connects the left and right hemisphere', as well as alterations to information processing centres of the brain which deal with language, facial recognition, and other tasks (Henrich, 2020, p. 3). In societies in which the ability to read became prevalent over the last millennium and most kin-based ties were removed, most notably in Western Europe and other countries where Europeans from WEIRD societies settled such as the US, broadly speaking, people became analytical thinkers and stopped thinking holistically (Henrich, 2020, pp. 54–55). This cultural shift co-evolved with physical changes in the brain. For instance, studies of brain activity reveal that in highly literate cultures facial recognition occurs in the right hemisphere, but in cultures in which most people are illiterate it takes place across both hemispheres (Henrich, 2020, p. 4). This correlates with an evolutionary shift from holistic to analytical thinking which continues to spread as humans move to urban settings where they live among strangers and gain more access to education.

Understanding this last point is important for IR because it has influenced, in important ways, relations between the globally dominant WEIRD cultures and the rest of the world. The enhanced ability to analyse gave WEIRD societies advantages over non-WEIRD cultures, for instance in the development of new forms of science and technology. The lapsing of kin-based ties in favour of interactions with strangers in cities allowed institutions and forms of social interaction to develop which depend on trust-based interactions with strangers, such as democratic elections and stock markets. Such advantages enabled some groups of Europeans to dominate and colonise many of the other cultures. However, the efforts of WEIRD nations to diffuse norms which have become established in the West (such as Western-style democracy and individual human rights) to non-WEIRD nations may have failed in some cases in part because of the culture–gene co-evolved differences between the West and the still kin-based traditional societies. For instance, this may explain, at least to a large extent, why Western-style democratic and legal institutions did not take root in Afghanistan during the US occupation from 2001 to 2021 (Ansary, 2010, p. 352).

Of course, not all of this is completely new. Theorists have previously proposed differences between cultures along a spectrum from collectivist to individualist (Hofstede & Hofstede, 2005) or from 'tight' to 'loose' (Gelfand et al., 2011). But the theory of culture–gene co-evolution is the first attempt to explain such differences in terms of an evolutionary framework, making it a more dynamic model which accounts for past changes, present-day relations between nations, and the possibility of future change. For instance, it is becoming clear that the divide between WEIRD and non-WEIRD societies – which itself to an extent is a construction occluding differences within and between peoples both in and outside Europe – is disappearing as traditional societies urbanise, industrialise, and gain access to modern education. This demonstrates how evolution can explain certain aspects of social change in conditions of globalisation. The science of culture–gene co-evolution includes rich and copious evidence from brain scans, palaeontology, DNA analysis, historical documents (for instance concerning edicts of the Catholic church), and psychological and economic experiments, rather than relying on just the survey data used by previous researchers in the social sciences (Gelfand et al., 2011; Hofstede & Hofstede, 2005).

At the same time, it is important not to overstate the implications of this research for IR. One has to be careful not to fall into the trap of oversimplifying cultural differences or falling back on straightforward linear causality. The path of human evolution, like human societies themselves, is full of non-linearity, feedback effects, and emergent phenomena. Accordingly, it is essential to put evolution (and co-evolution) in the context of complex systems analysis. As Erika Cudworth and Stephen Hobden (2011, p. 75) put it:

> What we call the international is a complex interweave of numerous systems nested, intersected and embedded in each other, all undergoing processes of co-evolution and linked by innumerable feedback loops. ... The study of complexity may provide an answer to the question of why international relations as a discipline has found it so hard to make progress, as this is a complex system with many subsystems interacting in multiple ways, and the developments in one can have impacts right across the system.

In other words, one has to find a way to apply culture–gene co-evolution within a complexity framework that takes account of the parallel co-evolutionary forces of social (socio-political) and natural (bio-physical) forces. As feminist IR scholar Elina Penttinen (2013) points out, biology and culture are intertwined, with implications for human politics as well as gender issues. Human agency cannot be discounted as one seeks to explain how societies and actors shape their futures ideationally as well as physically, rather than just being shaped by forces within them. People are both part of nature and able to act upon it. International relations between states are made up of an ever-fluctuating intersection of human-shaped attempts to act upon the world and unconscious motivations driven by biological forces.

Be all this as it may, the culture–gene co-evolution model has a solid body of evidence behind it and is suggestive of fruitful directions for research in IR. If culture–gene co-evolution has shaped aspects of the history of human societies in important ways, then logically it is necessary to examine precisely how this has influenced relations among groups of humans, including modern nation states. Among the issues important to IR which are influenced by culture–gene co-evolution are questions of norms, ethics, hierarchies, status, intergroup competition, and in-group cohesion. These will be examined in the following sections.

Key Takeaways

- *Cultural shifts drive specific aspects of genetic evolution in humans in a process called 'culture–gene co-evolution'.*
- *For instance, over centuries, widespread literacy in Europe thickened the connecting tissue between the left and right hemispheres of the brain, altering the brain areas which deal with language and facial recognition.*

- *As a result, culture–gene co-evolution has produced measurable differences between people from WEIRD societies and those from more traditional kin-based cultures. Most notably, it produced analytic as opposed to holistic thinking.*
- *This has implications for IR in terms of understanding relations between the West and the rest, and analysing the ongoing impacts of the colonial era and post-colonialism.*

5.3 Self-domestication

Self-domestication may seem like an odd concept. While there is no doubt that humans have domesticated once-wild animals such as wolves (which became dogs), aurochs (which became cattle), cats, sheep, chickens, and even bees, it seems strange that we would have somehow unconsciously domesticated ourselves. Yet there is copious scientific evidence to suggest that this is indeed what has happened. It has taken place through a process of culture–gene evolution over many generations and is continuing today. As humans have developed complex societies requiring ever-increasing cooperation among ever-larger groups of unrelated individuals, traits which promote such cooperation have become more common. On the other hand, traits which obstruct social cooperation, such as excessive violence or criminality, have become less common, often being removed from the gene pool through the execution of uncooperative individuals who disrupt the social order (Wrangham, 2019).

The domestication of animals entailed encouraging more cooperative, less aggressive traits to appear so that animals and humans could co-habit productively. Often, genetic modification occurred through selective breeding; but there has also been genetic evolution arising from adaptation. It has been demonstrated that wild animals become tame within a few generations, the descendants distinguished from their grandparents by becoming compliant, less aggressive, and adapted to living among humans (Wrangham, 2019, p. 70). Domesticated animals are physically as well as behaviourally quite different from their forebears. They are less prone to violence but also have physical characteristics that their ancestors did not have, such as different shaped ears and eyes, or different fur colourings (Wrangham, 2019, pp. 71–72). The difference with humans is that domestication took place through the evolution of traits that enabled us to co-habit and cooperate with other humans in groups and in domestic environments.

Richard Wrangham outlines a range of evidence for human self-domestication. He notes, for instance, that human self-domestication follows the same physical pattern as domestication in other animals:

> [T]he faces of domesticated animals tend to be shorter, projecting relatively less forward, than those of their wild ancestors. Teeth also become smaller, and jaws smaller still. ... Humans follow the same patterns. A study in the Sudan, where people lived continuously for the last ten thousand years, showed that faces became consistently shorter during that time. The trend began much earlier, however; for one, the first *Homo sapiens* had smaller faces than pre-*sapiens* species such as *Homo erectus*. Decline of tooth size has been noticed over the last hundred thousand years.... The rates of decline were similar in many areas across Europe, the Middle East, China, and Southeast Asia. (Wrangham, 2019, p. 62)

He also notes that males 'become less exaggeratedly male', with fewer physical differences between males and females (Wrangham, 2019, p. 63).

In terms of behaviour, Wrangham suggests that humans have become steadily less violent over time, and therefore more capable of cooperation. This development is crucial for developing complex societies containing thousands or millions of individuals. Excessive aggression is not conducive to harmonious social relations, particularly with strangers. Instead, increased levels of tolerance of others are required, which have been gained through long-term processes of self-domestication. At the same time, Wrangham claims that through increasing cooperation and reduced violence within the group, humans have become capable of increased levels of premeditated, organised violence against other groups. In other words, self-domestication has made us better able to cooperate within groups, but ironically also better able to inflict organised mass violence against other groups. As evolutionary biologists Hare and Woods (2020, p. xx, 19/257 in e-book) put it:

> When we feel that the group we love is threatened by a different social group, we are capable of unplugging the threatening group from our mental network – which allows us to dehumanize them. Where empathy and compassion would have been, there is nothing. Incapable of empathizing with threatening outsiders, we can't see them as fellow humans and become capable of the worst forms of cruelty. We are both the most tolerant and the most merciless species on the planet.

In other words, due to a process of evolutionary self-domestication, there has been a reduction in the tendency to *reactive aggression* – spontaneous, unpremeditated violence in reaction to immediate stimuli – but an increase in the capacity for *instrumental aggression* – premeditated violence coordinated among cooperating individuals.

For IR, the conclusions are obvious. Self-domestication, the taming of aggressive traits and physical characteristics, has enabled in-group cooperation and ultimately the formation of large, complex societies containing multitudes of strangers living in close proximity and performing a wide range of roles. At the same time, the increased cooperation which has resulted from self-domestication has produced the capacity, when combined with dramatic improvements in technology and weapons, for coordinating large-scale mass violence against other competing groups. The advent of technology and tools about 5,000 years ago (during the so-called bronze age) has given humanity a far greater potential for organised warfare. Our evolutionary history of self-domestication, as Richard Wrangham demonstrates, has made us both more and less violent, depending on the context (Hare, 2017; Hare & Woods, 2020; Wrangham, 2019). Any attempt to develop a normative approach to international affairs which would aim to mitigate the human tendency to intergroup warfare therefore needs to grapple with the implications of our history of self-domestication, increased in-group cooperation, and the subsequent potential for organised violence against competing groups.

Key Takeaways

- *Humans have self-domesticated, meaning that they have evolved traits which reduce physical aggression and promote in-group cooperation.*
- *This development has enabled the formation of large, complex, urbanised societies in which people with no kin relationship are able to interact.*
- *It has also created human societies equipped with scientifically advanced military technology and capable of coordinated violence against other groups on a scale not seen before in history.*

5.4 The Evolution of Language, Status, and Hierarchy

One distinctive and highly significant evolved human ability is language. The evolution of language is one of the adaptations which distinguishes us from our ape ancestors. Language enabled our ancestors to communicate and coordinate food gathering activity in order to survive in potentially harsh environments once they had emerged from the jungle in which they, like other primates, evolved. Individuals operating alone or with insufficient coordination between group members would not have been able to survive on the savanna and other hostile environments into which early humans migrated in search of food, and to which they were not directly biologically adapted. Survival depended on close in-group cooperation, which demanded the sharing of information and the allocation of roles within the group. Out of this cooperation language emerged once our brains and bodies had evolved sufficiently to enable speech to occur. As Turner (2021, p. 126) puts it:

> Once an animal can engage in speech, it can begin to accumulate and pass down cultural knowledge, ideas, moral codes, technologies, and other symbolic systems of information that then begin to supplement genetically driven tendencies to behave and organize in particular ways.

The precise origins and evolution of language are still under debate and information is scarce due to the difficulty of finding artefacts or fossils which would present evidence. However, a solid estimate is that language presumably evolved at least 150,000–200,000 years ago, when anatomically modern *Homo sapiens* appeared (Pagel, 2017).

The ability to speak has aspects which are both physical and sociocultural. Physically, there is the evolved capacity for the larynx, throat, tongue, and mouth to produce coherent, connected speech (Vince, 2019, pp. 91–92). Socioculturally, language evolved to be used for a complex and intertwined set of purposes, including storytelling, gossip, social bonding, and general promotion of cooperation (Storr, 2021, pp. 43–44). Among these cultural behaviours, gossip seems at first sight to be a rather trivial human trait with no possible bearing on international politics. However, researchers now believe that it plays a key role in the cohesion of human groups since it is connected to questions of status, reputation, and morality, all of which provide groups with the cohesion, stability, and structure they need to function. As Gaia Vince puts it, 'gossip is an essential tool for policing our interdependent societies, bringing wrongdoers and selfish and antisocial people into line, and making sure everyone in the group is pulling their weight' (Vince, 2019, p. 119). Will Storr (2021, p. 44) explains that

> one of gossip's critical purposes was to demonstrate the rules of the tribe and what happened if you broke them. By gossiping we demonstrate our knowledge of the rules, and our loyalty to them, and this can also earn status.

In other words, gossip plays a key role in enforcing moral codes, conformity to the group, and establishing status among the members. Gossip can result in loss of reputation, which has dire consequences for individuals exiled or ostracised, since without the support of the group they – and their genes – are highly unlikely to survive unless they can find another group which will accept them. As a result, 'status concerns are universal, operating in both men and women and in individuals in diverse cultures' (Anderson et al., 2015, p. 592). A psychological study of over 60,000 individuals in 123 countries (Tay & Diener, 2011) showed that the relative degree to which an individual attains respect is 'the strongest predictor of long-term positive and negative feelings' (Anderson et al., 2015, p. 580). In many countries, the 'loss of reputation is the most common reason people take their own lives' (Storr, 2021, p. 46). Thus, 'the relevant evidence suggests that the desire for status is indeed fundamental' (Anderson et al., 2015, p. 574). This implies that gossip, far from being just idle tittle-tattle, is in fact a key function of language as an assessment of reputation. Through gossip and reputation, conformity to social norms and practices is enforced, enabling the group to become more cohesive and hence able to compete with (or out-compete) rival groups.

Storytelling is another way in which humans bind the collective together and enhance the chances of individuals acquiring skills needed to promote individual and group survival. Stories perform this function by acting as a tool for elder members of the group to communicate vital cultural knowledge and norms (Storr, 2021, p. 44). Our brains find it difficult to absorb information through simple instructions or lists, and stories have been shown to be vastly more effective tools for imparting knowledge (Bruner, 1987). This is because, as Gaia Vince (2019, p. 69) puts it,

> [s]tories work as a cultural memory bank because the narrative device provides contextual 'infrastructure' that helps us understand, organize, share and store factual information. ... Our brains react as though we were living the story and experiencing it firsthand. In this way, a storyteller can implant emotions, thoughts and ideas into the minds of the audience, making them feel as though they are experiencing the same events. In fact, scans show that the storyteller and the listeners' brains actually start to synchronize during storytelling – neurologists describe it as 'speaker-listener neural coupling'.

In other words, evolution has equipped us with brains that light up when supplied with narratives rather than instructions – all in the service of promoting the survival of the group by ensuring that vital cultural knowledge, social practices, rituals, and routinised behaviour are passed on through generations.

As far as in-group and intergroup dynamics are concerned, the consequence of close in-group cohesion based on gossip, rituals, and storytelling is that non-conformers and outsiders are viewed as having incorrect norms and behaviours. This strengthens in-group cooperation against other groups, but at the same time encourages intolerance and the potential for coordinated violence against those perceived as enemies. Loyalty to the collective promotes the interests of the group and encourages the close cohesion needed to outcompete other groups. At the same time, it creates the conditions for intergroup warfare by making individuals capable of violence, self-sacrifice, and even death for the well-being of the band, tribe, or nation. All such traits emerge from culture–gene co-evolution as humans acquired the physical hardware – better brains and larynxes – to produce language, enabling more sophisticated in-group cooperation and simultaneously developing increasingly complex cultural norms. In other words, human in-group cooperation and intergroup competition are closely connected to the evolution of language, status, hierarchy, and morality as cultural traits promoting group survival. Such traits also constitute the evolved basis of what we now refer to as relations between states and dynamics within human collectives.

Michelle Murray (2019) demonstrates in a book-length study that the universal human quest for enhanced status and reputation extends to complex human collectives such as nation states, acting along the same lines as individuals. Like individuals, as nations become aware of their status relative to other states, they begin to seek displays of respect from the international community and to improve their position in the international hierarchy. When such respect is lacking, and a nation feels it is not being designated the status that it deserves, it may seek to gain respect through conspicuous demonstrations of wealth or even by waging war. For instance, Murray demonstrates through a case study of Germany in the late nineteenth and early twentieth centuries that the country's path to war arose from a national feeling that it was not being given the respect and status it merited. This, she shows, accounts for the German pursuit of naval power and colonies: it was done not primarily to win a war but to try to force other nations, especially Britain, to recognise Germany's high status in the international order and give it the appropriate standing in discussions of colonial affairs. When this search for recognition did not win Britain's respect, and instead suspicions rose on each side accompanied by an arms race, the result was that the two countries formed rival alliances, producing the conditions which triggered the First World War (Murray, 2019, p. 139). On the other hand, America's rise to global power in the first half of the twentieth century ultimately earned Britain's acceptance and routinised recognition (after some initial resistance), producing a peaceful power transition from Britain to the US (Murray, 2019, p. 189).

Another aspect of social evolution and the quest for status is the development of hierarchies. Hierarchy within groups emerged from a combination of social complexification and the fact of some bands and tribes gaining access to rich resources, which then became concentrated in the hands of a few members of the group (Testot, 2020, p. 48). Apes have been shown to be not as strictly hierarchical as monkeys, but it is inevitable that hierarchies will form when status and reputation are important aspects of interpersonal dynamics (Turner, 2021, pp. 116–119). Clearly, individuals with higher status gain more opportunities to reproduce, meaning that their genes have a much higher chance of survival: the famous case of this is Genghis Khan, who is said to be the ancestor of millions of people across Asia. In this we are not dissimilar to our primate relatives, in that

> dominant male[s] monopolize access to the females, pushing the other males to the margins of the group. It is associated with strategies for alliances and fights for dominance ... systematic monopolization by males may well be imprinted into our genes. (Testot, 2020, p. 19)

Thus, despite the prognostications of some prominent scholarly voices advocating anarchism or anarcho-syndicalism (Chomsky, 1989; Graeber, 2004), it is difficult to see how complex modern societies containing millions of members could function without hierarchical and status-based elements in which some individuals are accorded greater respect than others.

In the international sphere, hierarchies appeared when states began to compete with each other without necessarily going to war, creating a society of states in which some dominated others, demanding higher status and respect. For instance, David Kang (2012) points out that the East Asian international system was for centuries (before Europeans arrived) founded on a tribute-based hierarchy with China at the centre. In the contemporary era, despite the influential neorealist assertion that the international system is anarchic (Waltz, 1979), there are distinct hierarchical elements. States are not equal since some have far greater influence than others. Examples include the veto power of the five permanent members in the UN Security Council and the US influence over the global financial system via supposedly multilateral institutions such as the World Bank and the International Monetary Fund, which have their headquarters in the US. In Europe, economically powerful nations such as Germany, France, and Britain clearly have more clout than others, and the same can be said of Russia, China, India, and Japan in Asia.

In an ideational sense, states at or near the top of the global hierarchy expect signs of respect from those lower down such as deference to their normative requirements. As an example, the European Union sees itself as a 'normative power' (Manners, 2002). The assumption that other nations lower down the pecking order will recognise the EU's status in the global hierarchy leads to the assumption that they will listen and conform to its agendas concerning democracy and human rights, even if 'European values' based on individualism do not necessarily match the cultural norms of kin-based societies. Similarly, the US, Russia, and China (all permanent members of the UN Security Council) automatically expect other nations – especially those over which they have influence – to defer to them and conform to their wishes. The cost of disrespect may be threats, sanctions, or military invasion. Examples include the Russian invasion of Ukraine in 2022 and the American demonisation of Iran since the humiliation of the 1979 US embassy hostage crisis. These nations may not realise that they are demanding respect for their status and may instead claim to believe that they are promoting universal ethical agendas; but national pride and the demand for recognition undoubtedly play a key role in their behaviour and attitudes.

On a slightly different note, the Chinese government uses what it terms the 'century of humiliation' (suffered at the hands of Europeans in the nineteenth century) to mobilise its population in the service of fulfilling a national dream of renewed self-respect, as well as increased status in the eyes of other nations (Brown, 2018; Callahan, 2010). This appears to be a case where status seems to turn in upon itself, with prestige being dependent on self-recognition as much as on the recognition of others. Yet still the Chinese sense of humiliation, used by the government as a tool to motivate national pride and productivity, is about China's reduced standing in the community of nations, among which it long saw itself as the 'Middle Kingdom' (which is the approximate meaning of China's name for itself, *zhongguo*) during its imperial era. Thus, China's 'economic miracle' since Deng Xiaoping's reforms in the 1980s is driven by a vision of renewed self-respect as well as restoring itself to a high, perhaps dominant, position in global society (Garlick, 2024).

In short, the search for status, respect, and recognition is a key part of human evolved psychology. This is the case because it promotes the interests and survival of the individual and the group. Status and recognition connect to language and morality, and all these cultural traits are connected to the cultural-genetic co-evolution of the brain. As far as IR are concerned, nations act like individuals, seeking recognition for their status and jockeying for position in the hierarchy of states. Just as with individuals, when nations feel that they are not being awarded sufficient respect by other actors, the results can be catastrophic for all concerned. While it is not the case that all wars result from what Murray (2019) calls the 'struggle for recognition', this has undoubtedly been the cause for some. Most notably, it can be posited as the underlying cause of the First and Second World Wars: these arguably stemmed from Germany and Japan trying to build empires to gain their place in the sun next to the existing colonial powers such as Britain. In this sense, the human search for status and respect, so critical in our evolutionary heritage, can be viewed as an integral – and inevitable – part of relations between states, influencing outcomes and competition between them.

Key Takeaways

- *Language evolved to enable in-group cooperation. Gossip and storytelling emerged as cultural functions of language which enforce conformity to moral codes and norms, as well as establishing status and hierarchy among the members.*
- *Hierarchy within groups emerged from social complexification and resources being controlled by a few powerful individuals. International hierarchies emerged from interstate competition for status and recognition, which have caused the outbreaks of at least some major wars.*

5.5 Norms, Morality, and Religion

The idea that ethics, morality, and religion have a genetic basis is a hard pill for many social scientists to swallow. What Darwinian social scientists call 'the standard social science model' is based on

> the idea that biology doesn't much matter – that the uniquely malleable human mind, together with the unique force of culture, has severed our behavior from its evolutionary roots; that there is no inherent human nature driving human events. (Wright, 1996, p. 5)

Yet, as evolutionary psychologists Jonathan Haidt and Robert Wright show, this model is incorrect. There are solid scientific reasons to believe that morality evolved from in-group interactions to serve as the psychological-emotional glue which binds societies together. As such, morality and religious beliefs can be understood as key aspects of human nature emerging from culture–gene co-evolution rather than products of some kind of divine spark arising in blank-slate minds concerning values, what is 'right', and what is 'true'. As Wright (1996, p. 12) puts it:

> Altruism, compassion, empathy, love, conscience, the sense of justice – all of these things, the things that hold society together, the things that allow our species to think so highly of itself, can now confidently be said to have a firm genetic basis.

Haidt concurs that 'morality is the extraordinary human capacity that made civilization possible' (Haidt, 2012, p. xii). Revealingly, as Robert Wright documents, Charles Darwin (who apart from being a naturalist was an Anglican parson) himself experienced a lifelong struggle to acknowledge the evolutionary role of religion and morality in the context of his Christian faith (Wright, 1996).

The previous section outlined the evolution of language, status, and culture. It should be clear by now, however difficult or distasteful it may be for some to accept, that norms, morality, and even religious beliefs and rituals are part of the same package of culture–gene evolution as other phenomena. Norms, practices, and rituals, although common to all human societies and possessing many general similarities, often differ between cultures quite dramatically, distinguishing groups from one another. They emerge from the complexification of society over millennia and the need to develop behaviours and attitudes promoting the cohesion and prosperity of the group so that it is able to compete with (or outcompete) other groups. Norms and rituals, for instance concerning age-based hierarchies, ancestor burial, inheritance, and marriage, serve to 'foster tightly knit units with clear lines of authority' (Henrich, 2020, p. 105). In an example of this, the anthropologist Donald Tuzin conducted an ethnographic study of hunter-gatherer societies in New Guinea. He found that by successfully integrating subgroups through ritualistic practices, one community outcompeted others in a region in which military and economic threats had proliferated. In the process, the successful group became far larger than the others and evolved more complex social and political practices, fostering enhanced cooperation between previously disparate subgroups and enabling it to dominate the region (Tuzin, 2001).

In other words, for hunter-gatherer societies to increase in size, outcompete other groups, and foster enhanced in-group cooperation and cohesion, there was a need for rituals and practices which would gain religious and moral significance in order to bind several previously competing groups together into a larger entity. This process of developing socially binding rituals, customs, moral codes, and religions subsequently contributed to the development of larger, more complex societies which could function effectively and form larger polities. These, especially as they grew in size, had the capacity to mobilise coordinated military activity on a greater scale than had previously been possible in groups of 300 or fewer individuals. Eventually, in the context of population growth and the advent of agriculture, this led to ever-increasing intergroup competition, which resulted in the creation of large, complex societies consisting of thousands, then hundreds of thousands, then millions of individuals. Large complex societies of this type also required centralised governmental institutions to run them, since familial or communal decision-making would obviously no longer be practical (Diamond, 1997, pp. 286–288).

For IR, what this means is that the norms and rituals specific to a society should be reinterpreted as being the cement binding the building blocks of complex societies together. Language, culture, empathy, morality, and religion forge a spirit of connectedness within groups that is essential for persuading individuals to work together for the sake of the collective. In this way,

> we develop the idea of belonging, of 'us' and 'them'. And also the idea of 'us' *against* 'them'. ... [E]volution has produced in us this need to be close to some and to compare with and confront ourselves against others. (Testot, 2020, p. 29, italics in original)

The social phenomena we call 'morality' and 'religion' thus have both positive and negative aspects: positive in the sense that they bind us together and enable large masses of people to cooperate in the service of complex national goals, but negative in the sense that they facilitate coordinated violence towards other competing groups. One needs only to think of the long history of bloody violence against other peoples justified with reference to group ideologies, moral codes, civilisational values, or religions to realise that this is so. Examples from the last millennium – with varying levels of emotional trigger depending on the reader's viewpoint and distance in time from the events – might include the Medieval Crusades to the Holy Land, the Spanish conquest of the Americas, European colonialism (with its notorious 'white man's burden'), the Nazi Holocaust, or the US 'war on terror' against the 'axis of evil'.

What is generally not acknowledged is that the tendency to use religion and culture in the service of warfare is part of our evolved psychology. Putting it another way, intergroup competition and conflict in which religion, morality, or nationalism are used as part of the justification are an evolved part of human nature rather than being explained away (as they often are) as some kind of aberration stemming from 'evil' individuals leading their nations into error. It is only by recognising this fact that human beings can hope to channel their evolved psychology into more beneficial, productive, or at least less harmful forms of intergroup competition (such as international sports competitions followed by large portions of the citizenry or companies competing for customers), instead of inflicting violence on members of other groups.

Key Takeaways

- *Morality and religion evolved to bind individuals in societies together. They foster a collective spirit which promotes group survival through coordinated action against other groups.*
- *Intergroup competition and conflict justified through religion, morality, or nationalism are cultural aspects of evolved human nature.*

5.6 Intergroup Competition and In-Group Cooperation

The preceding sections have revealed the significance of intergroup competition and in-group cooperation in human evolutionary history. Without effective in-group cooperation, individuals or families would not have been able to survive in the many different environments into which the growing human population dispersed across the world. Dividing tasks in the group (such as hunting, gathering, child-rearing, and making clothes) enabled groups to survive in what would have previously been hostile environments. It is through in-group cooperation and cohesion that human groups have managed to inhabit almost every type of environment from relatively arid to fertile, and from extremely hot to extremely cold.

An important part of in-group cooperation is the evolutionary role of caring and empathy towards both relatives and non-relatives. Recent research into group selection suggests that the survival of the in-group can be promoted by altruistic behaviour towards non-relatives (Mayseless, 2016, p. 21). At the same time, hostility towards out-groups (in-group/out-group bias) remains an inherited trait, although coalitions between groups may be evolutionarily advantageous if common cause can be found (Mayseless, 2016, p. 23). Caring for others may be seen as a part of evolved self-domestication, even leading to intergroup cooperation according to the principle of 'survival of the friendliest' (Hare, 2017; Hare & Woods, 2020).

As far as IR is concerned, one of the most important findings of researchers is that intergroup competition drives enhanced in-group cooperation (Francois et al., 2018; Haidt, 2012; Henrich, 2004). Violent conflicts over territory and resources have occurred throughout human history, and fighting them successfully demands cohesion and coordination within the group (Haidt, 2012, p. 252). To promote bonding, collective institutions, norms, practices, and rituals are adopted, sometimes copied from more successful groups. This leads to the formation of more successful and more complex societies: larger societies have significant competitive advantages over smaller ones in terms of division and diversification of labour, as well as the ability to mobilise larger armies and produce innovative military and other technologies. The long-term process in which complex hierarchical societies evolve due to intergroup conflict has been termed *group selection* (Turchin et al., 2013; Turchin & Gavrelets, 2009).

It needs to be emphasised that in-group cooperation in complex societies requires the presence of competing groups to foster a sense of unity. In the absence of competition, group cohesion disintegrates due to internal disagreements:

> Once intergroup competition wanes, which often happens when states or empires manage to eliminate their competition, things slowly fall apart. Without the looming threats posed by competing societies, the competition among ruling families within a society will intensify and gradually tear the state-level institutions apart. Cracks, gaps, and loopholes appear even in the best institutions, allowing narrow elite interests to flood in, as lineages, clans, and sometimes entire ethnic communities devise ways to exploit state institutions for their own ends. (Henrich, 2020, p. 120)

The result of such in-group dissonance in the absence of competing rival groups can be civil wars or splintering into subgroups, drastically weakening what was once an all-conquering empire or state. An example of this would be the Roman empire, which had become completely dominant in the Mediterranean region by the birth of Christ. Since it had no enemies of anything resembling a similar size, the lack of external competition meant that Rome was instead beset by internal power struggles and social decay which weakened it by the fifth century CE. These divisions caused the empire to split into rival Western and Eastern versions of itself and allowed tribes which seemed to lack its advantages to ransack the city of Rome itself.

The lesson here for IR is clear. Any attempt to advocate peace and cooperation between nations needs to contain an element of competition to satisfy the demands of evolutionary psychology. Without it, things fall apart, as they did between the First and Second World Wars. The effort to maintain peace through discussions in the League of Nations failed because it expected nations to establish a 'harmony of interests' that was not compatible with the drive for power (Carr, 1981). Putting this in evolutionary terms, the belief that nations could cooperate rather than compete ran counter to evolved human psychology in terms of the drivers of in-group cohesion.

Thus, according to evolutionary psychology, intergroup competition can be seen as an inevitable part of the human experience which cannot be entirely overcome or eliminated due to its co-evolved cultural-genetic basis. Humans are driven by measuring themselves against others, either within the group as they jostle for status and hierarchy, or between groups as nations similarly jostle for status and hierarchy in international society. For this reason, it would be better to foster more benign forms of intergroup competition (such as international sports competitions or companies competing for business) to undercut the worst excesses of human evolutionary psychology through a form of what might be termed *conflict substitution*. Indeed, one study found that increased competition between firms produced higher levels of cooperation and trust. Firms which managed to generate enhanced cooperation between employees outcompeted their rivals and, in a process of group selection, firms with greater internal cooperation proliferated, while ones with lower levels of cooperation disappeared from the marketplace (Francois et al., 2018).

Thus, it is feasible that human evolutionary psychology may be directed towards more productive (or at least less destructive) channels of activity than intergroup warfare. As self-domesticating humans find more and more new, alternative means of vying for status while expressing competitive instincts (such as computer games, singing and dancing contests, or even the social media search for 'likes' and followers), it is possible that this may lead to a reduction in the incidence of violent intra- and intergroup conflict; this can take place along similar lines (although using different means) to the solution adopted by our evolutionary cousins the bonobos. Indeed, arguably sports and other intergroup competitions have already served a role as conflict substitution to an ever-increasing extent since the industrial revolution. The expanding roster of international events such as the Olympics, the football World Cup, the Eurovision Song Contest, and so on provides evidence of the proliferation of non-violent outlets for in-group solidarity (among supporters) against out-group rivals. International competitions today occur on an exponentially greater scale, especially in industrial and post-industrial urbanised societies, than one or two centuries ago. The ongoing addition of more such outlets provides evidence of an ongoing evolutionary process of self-domesticating conflict substitution which demands further research and more data than are available at the time of writing this Element.

In short, there is a need for IR to address questions of human nature (as classical realists such as Niebuhr (1941) and Morgenthau (1948) once did), evolutionary psychology, and culture–gene co-evolution in order to search for fuller explanations for problems that have stirred heated debate between scholars since the advent of the IR discipline in the early twentieth century. Intergroup competition and in-group cooperation have a basis in our evolutionary history which is not at first sight obvious but needs to be acknowledged in order to develop sounder normative approaches to the problems of IR such as wars and other forms of intergroup conflict and cooperation. This can perhaps be achieved by encouraging further forms of conflict substitution and self-domesticated culture–gene co-evolution to reduce the tendency for intergroup violence (Hare & Woods, 2020).

Key Takeaways

- *Evolved in-group cooperation allowed humans to survive in hostile environments and against competing groups.*
- *Intergroup competition is a key driver of in-group cooperation and cohesion, creating increasingly complex societies as culture and technology evolve.*
- *Theory and practice in IR need to take account of evolved human psychology concerning in-group cooperation and intergroup competition.*

6 Conclusion

The preceding pages have presented some implications of evolutionary science for the field of IR. Sections 3 and 4 revealed the field's lack of attention to evolutionary psychology and culture–gene co-evolution as drivers of international phenomena such as in-group cooperation and competition with other groups. Sections 4 and 5 outlined the importance of findings from evolutionary theory, evolutionary psychology, and neuroscience for IR. The following are the most important findings.

First and foremost, humans have co-evolved cultural and genetic traits which encourage in-group cooperation driven by competition with out-groups (Waring

& Wood, 2021). This implies that identifying with one's in-group and the 'othering' of individuals from other groups are inherited characteristics. They, and the violent conflicts that often ensue as a result of them, are not an aberration or 'evil' that we humans can overcome. They are imprinted into us as key drivers of our behaviour, emotions, and attitudes. For IR, this means that intergroup competition is an ineluctable part of human experience that cannot be removed from the picture however much some would like that to happen. Competition and conflict between groups drive in-group cohesion and cooperation in a process called group selection (Turchin & Gavrelets, 2009). In its absence, researchers have found that in-group cohesion collapses and conflicts break out between factions within the group (Henrich, 2020, p. 120). Normatively, this means that it is desirable to focus on productive rather than destructive forms of intergroup competition. Such competition can be achieved through benign international rivalries in spheres such as economics, sport, and the status connected to these, rather than letting the human tendency to organise mass violence against other groups have free rein. Understanding the point that competition with other groups is a part of our evolved psychological heritage is a key finding of this Element as far as IR is concerned.

Another key finding is that we cannot separate ourselves from our primate past (de Waal, 2005). It is an intrinsic part of who we are, much as we like to assume that we have outgrown or overcome our 'animal' traits. For instance, emotions play a key role in decision-making, meaning that the rational actor model (based on an in-built assumption of human exceptionalism) prevalent in IR needs to be revised (Gammon, 2020; Lerner et al., 2015). Given the imperatives of evolved human nature, it is not easy (perhaps impossible for most people) to behave differently than how their culture–gene co-evolution causes them to behave. Normatively, this means that we cannot overcome who we are, but we can attempt to guide our evolved characteristics in benign rather than violent directions in the international sphere. As humans with primate-derived characteristics, we are (in a holistic sense) all in it together regardless of our national allegiances and cultures, with shared genetic heritage that makes us behave in similar ways, including the inevitable competition with other groups and close identification with the culture and language of an in-group.

In this context, there are other important points to be noted. The idea of co-evolved culture–gene differences between WEIRD societies and the rest of the world presents a new viewpoint on the past and present of IR which provides a deeper understanding of the long-term causes and consequences of European imperialism and colonialism. The body of evidence demonstrates that the activity of the Catholic church in Europe led, over centuries, to the removal of kin-based ties in large family groups in favour of nuclear families driven to trust-based cooperation with strangers in urban settings. In addition, the influence of the Protestant church through its emphasis on personal Bible study led to high levels of literacy, which produced discernible changes in the brain in favour of analytic over holistic thinking (Henrich, 2020). Taken together, analytic thinking and higher level of trust towards strangers created European societies which produced significant phenomena such as science and technology, stock markets, the industrial revolution, and national armies capable of conquering societies which culturally and genetically remained rooted in kin-based ties and holistic thinking. Today's international system, including the consequences of European imperialism and colonialism across the world, is thus based in co-evolved cultural-genetic differences between Europe and most of the rest of the world. However, as human evolution continues, it is likely that these cultural-genetic gaps between Europeans and non-Europeans are disappearing amidst increasingly widespread literacy and the advent of modern communications technology such as the internet. In short, the long-term implications of the changes wrought by WEIRD cultures in the international arena are still playing out and are highly important avenues for future research by scholars in both IR and other fields.

It also needs to be understood that the evolution of cultural traits distinct from other groups – such as religion, norms, morality, and language – is an in-group cohesion mechanism promoting the survival of the group, in some cases enabling it to out-compete other groups. Culture is universal to all human groups despite the clear differences which distinguish them one from another. Culture–gene co-evolution also occurs across all groups, with the evolution of different physical traits being evidence of this. Therefore, the role of culture in IR needs to be more emphasised and better understood than it is at present. Instead of emphasising supposedly impersonal forces represented by abstract concepts such as 'anarchy' and 'ontological security', IR scholars would be well advised to investigate the evolution and discernible impacts of specific cultural traits on relations between nations, based on the body of empirical evidence concerning these that is steadily emerging in evolutionary psychology, neuroscience, and other fields.

This is not to say that conceptual thinking is worthless; far from it. Rather, there is a need to build a more solid empirical support base for it. If, as Alexander Wendt (1992) suggested, anarchy is what states make of it, scholars need to remember what states are made of: human beings. Without understanding evolved human nature, one cannot fathom why conditions of anarchy or hierarchy come to exist. Supposedly 'independent variables' such as 'anarchy in the international system' do not exist in a vacuum free of human beings, but very much because human beings create the conditions for them to exist. The same can be said of 'ontological (in-)security'. Research in evolution can provide some of the tools for building a foundation for examining the human psychology which generates tensions and conflicts between states. Evolutionary science can provide an empirical basis which enriches the context within which conceptual thinking in IR takes place.

In short, as far as IR and evolution are concerned, the avenues for future research are many. This Element has only been able to introduce a few of the most significant ones; there are certainly many others. The analysis presented is intended to be an introduction to the importance of evolution for IR, laying a foundation for more detailed research in the future than was possible here. Evidence from evolutionary science has the potential to transform research in IR in important ways that should be seen as enriching rather than undermining the field, presenting the opportunity to develop radically enhanced understandings of how human societies such as nation states evolve their identities and interact with each other.

At the same time, researchers need to be wary of the consequences of possible misapplications of scientific findings. In a field of study such as IR, with its focus on international politics and relations between nations, there is an ever-present potential for misunderstandings about sensitive issues such as race and gender (Jacobi & Freyberg-Inan, 2015, p. 12). The social Darwinist movement of the early twentieth century presents a stark warning of the negative consequences of misuse and abuse of scientific research. Researchers need to step carefully and apply evolutionary science in a nuanced fashion to avoid the possibility of their work being used to justify rather than ameliorate hatred and violence towards other groups. Overcoming stereotypes about other groups (and one's own group) is inherently difficult due to the evolved traits outlined in this Element.

In a world in which extremist politics appears to be on the rise, IR still needs to be aware of the pitfalls of abusing science. To repeat an old adage, the road to hell is paved with good intentions. Applying evolutionary science to IR therefore needs to be done with attention to areas of detail and with a clear understanding of the human tendency to use resources to promote in-group solidarity against perceived threats from out-groups. In other words, there is a high potential for evolutionary science itself – as happened in the past – to be used to support political agendas promoting hatred and violence. Researchers in IR and other fields need to be keenly aware of this potential and to steer a careful course around it as they use evolution to form new understandings of IR.

References

Abramitzky, R. (2018). *The Mystery of the Kibbutz: Egalitarian Principles in a Capitalist World*. Princeton: Princeton University Press.

Alexander, R. D. (1990). *How did humans evolve? Reflections on the uniquely unique species*. Museum of Zoology (Special publication no. 1), Ann Arbor: University of Michigan. https://hdl.handle.net/2027.42/57178.

Anderson, C., Hildreth, J. A. D., & Howland, L. (2015). Is the desire for status a fundamental human motive? A review of the empirical literature. *Psychological Bulletin*, 141(3): 574–601. https://doi.org/10.1037/a0038781.

Ansary, T. (2010). *Destiny Disrupted: A History of the World through Islamic Eyes*. New York: PublicAffairs.

Axelrod, R., & Keohane, R. O. (1985). Achieving cooperation under anarchy: Strategies and institutions. *World Politics*, 38(1): 226–254. https://doi.org/10.2307/2010357.

Barkin, J. S. (2003). Realist constructivism. *International Studies Review*, 5(3): 325–342. https://doi.org/10.1046/j.1079-1760.2003.00503002.x.

Barkin, S. (2010). *Realist Constructivism: Rethinking International Relations Theory*. Cambridge: Cambridge University Press.

Bieler, A., & Morton, A. D. (2004). A critical theory route to hegemony, world order and historical change: Neo-Gramscian perspectives in international relations. *Capital & Class*, 28(1): 85–113. https://doi.org/10.1057/9780230627307_2.

Boehm, C. (1999). *Hierarchy in the Forest: The Evolution of Egalitarian Behavior*. Cambridge, MA: Harvard University Press.

Bousquet, A., & Curtis, S. (2011). Beyond models and metaphors: Complexity theory, systems thinking and international relations. *Cambridge Review of International Affairs*, 24(1): 43–62. https://doi.org/10.1080/09557571.2011.558054.

Bowles, S. (2009). Did warfare among ancestral hunter-gatherers affect the evolution of human social behaviors? *Science*, 324(5932): 1293–1298. https://doi.org/10.1126/science.1168112.

Brown, C. (2013). 'Human nature', science and international political theory. *Journal of International Relations and Development*, 16(4): 435–454. https://doi.org/10.1057/jird.2013.17.

Brown, C. (2015). The Marxist perspective from "species-being" to natural justice. In Jacobi, D., & Freyberg-Inan, A. (eds.), *Human Beings in*

International Relations. Cambridge: Cambridge University Press, pp. 95–112.

Brown, K. (2018). *China's Dream: The Culture of Chinese Communism and the Secret Sources of Its Power*. Cambridge: Polity Press.

Bruner, J. (1987). *Actual Minds, Possible Worlds*. Cambridge, MA: Harvard University Press.

Bull, H. (1977). *The Anarchical Society: A Study of Order in World Politics*. London: Macmillan.

Buzan, B. (2004). *From International to World Society? English School Theory and the Social Structure of Globalization*. Cambridge: Cambridge University Press.

Buzan, B., & Acharya, A. (2022). *Re-imagining International Relations: World Orders in the Thought and Practice of Indian, Chinese, and Islamic Civilizations*. Cambridge: Cambridge University Press.

Callahan, W. A. (2010). *China: The Pessoptimist Nation*. Oxford: Oxford University Press.

Carey, N. (2012). *The Epigenetics Revolution: How Modern Biology is Rewriting Our Understanding of Genetics, Disease, and Inheritance*. New York: Columbia University Press.

Carr, E. H. (1981). *The Twenty Years' Crisis: 1919–1939: An Introduction to the Study of International Relations*, 2nd ed. London: Macmillan.

Chapman, J. W. (1975). Rawls's Theory of Justice. *American Political Science Review*, 69(2): 588–593. https://doi.org/10.2307/1959089.

Chomsky, N. (1989). Preface. In Rocker, R. (ed.), *Anarcho-Syndicalism*. London: Pluto Press, pp. vi–vii.

Christakis, N. A. (2019). *Blueprint: The Evolutionary Origin of a Good Society*. New York: Little, Brown, Spark.

Chudek, M., & Henrich, J. (2011). Culture–gene coevolution, norm-psychology and the emergence of human prosociality. *Trends in Cognitive Sciences*, 15(5): 218–226. https://doi.org/10.1016/j.tics.2011.03.003.

Corning, P. A. (2023). Culture–gene co-evolution: Darwin's other theory comes into view. *Biological Journal of the Linnean Society*, 139(4): 563–569. https://doi.org/10.1093/biolinnean/blac048.

Coveney, P., & Highfield, R. (1995). *Frontiers of Complexity: The Search for Order in a Chaotic World*. London: Faber and Faber.

Cox, R. W. (1981). Social forces, states and world orders: Beyond international relations theory. *Millennium*, 10(2): 126–155. https://doi.org/10.1177/03058298810100020501.

References

Cox, R. W. (1983). Gramsci, hegemony and international relations: An essay in method. *Millennium*, 12(2): 162–175. https://doi.org/10.1177/03058298830120020701.

Cox, R. W. (1987). *Production, Power and World Order: Social Forces in the Making of History*. New York: Columbia University Press.

Crawford, N. C. (2016). Studying world politics as a complex adaptive system. In Booth, K., & Erskine, T. (eds.), *International Relations Theory Today* (2nd ed.). Cambridge: Polity Press, pp. 263–267.

Cudworth, E., & Hobden, S. (2011). *Posthuman International Relations: Complexity, Ecologism and Global Politics*. London: Zed Books.

Damasio, A. (1994). *Descartes' Error*. New York: G.P. Putnam's Sons.

Damasio, A. (2000). *The Feeling of What Happens: Body, Emotion and the Making of Consciousness*. London: Vintage.

David-Barrett, T. (2023). Human group size puzzle: Why it is odd that we live in large societies. *Royal Society Open Science*, 10(8): 230559. https://doi.org/10.1098/rsos.230559.

Dehaene, S. (2009). *Reading in the Brain: The Science and Evolution of a Human Invention*. New York: Viking.

Dehaene, S., Pegado, F., Braga, L. W., et al. (2010). How learning to read changes the cortical networks for vision and language. *Science*, 330(6009): 1359–1364. https://doi.org/10.1126/science.1194140

Devetak, R. (2012). An introduction to international relations: The origins and changing agendas of a discipline. In Devetak, R., Burke, A., & George, J. (eds.), *An Introduction to International Relations* (2nd ed.). Cambridge: Cambridge University Press, pp. 1–19.

Devetak, R., Burke, A., & George, J. (eds.). *An Introduction to International Relations (2nd ed.)*. Cambridge: Cambridge University Press.

de Waal, F. (2005). *Our Inner Ape: The Best and Worst of Human Nature*. London: Granta.

Diamond, J. (1997). *Guns, Germs, and Steel: The Fates of Human Societies*. New York: W.W. Norton.

Dias, B. G., & Ressler, K. J. (2014). Parental olfactory experience influences behavior and neural structure in subsequent generations. *Nature Neuroscience*, 17(1): 89–96. https://doi.org/10.1038/nn.3594.

Dietl, G. P. (2008). Selection, security, and evolutionary international relations. In Sagarin, R. D., & Taylor, T. (eds.), *Natural Security: A Darwinian Approach to a Dangerous World*. Berkeley: University of California Press, pp. 86–101.

Diez, T. (2005). Constructing the Self and Changing Others: Reconsidering "Normative Power Europe." *Millennium*, 33(3): 613–636. https://doi.org/10.1177/03058298050330031701.

Edwards, J. (2009). *Language and Identity*. Cambridge: Cambridge University Press.

Ellison, T. M., & Reinöhl, U. (2022). Compositionality, Metaphor, and the Evolution of Language. *International Journal of Primatology*, 45: 703–719. https://doi.org/10.1007/s10764-022-00315-w.

Facundo, M., Sahakian, B., Clark, L., et al. (2002). Decision-making processes following damage to the prefrontal cortex. *Brain*, 125(3), 624–639. https://doi.org/10.1093/brain/awf049.

Forbes, A. A., & Krimmel, B. A. (2010). Evolution is change in the inherited traits of a population through successive generations. *Nature Education Knowledge*, 3(10): 6. www.nature.com/scitable/knowledge/library/evolution-is-change-in-the-inherited-traits-15164254/.

Foucault, M. (1984). *The Foucault Reader* (ed. Rabinow, P.). New York: Pantheon.

Francois, P., Fujiwara, T., & van Ypersele, T. (2018). The origins of human prosociality: Cultural group selection in the workplace and the laboratory. *Science Advances* 4: eaat2201. https://doi.org/10.1126/sciadv.aat2201.

Freeston, M. H., Rhéaume, J., Letarte, H., Dugas, M. J., & Ladouceur, R. (1994). Why do people worry? *Personality and Individual Differences*, 17(6): 791–802. https://doi.org/10.1016/0191-8869(94)90048-5.

Gammon, E. (2020). Affective neuroscience, emotional regulation, and international relations. *International Theory*, 12(2): 189–219. https://doi.org/10.1017/S1752971919000253.

Garlick, J. (2020a). Bringing human nature back in: The implications of neuroscience, psychology and evolution for international relations (IR) theory. *Academia Letters*, Article 84. https://doi.org/10.20935/AL84.

Garlick, J. (2020b). *The Impact of China's Belt and Road Initiative: From Asia to Europe*. Abingdon: Routledge.

Garlick, J. (2024). *Advantage China: Agent of Change in an Era of Global Disruption*. London: Bloomsbury.

Garlick, J., & Qin, F. (2023a). China's normative power in central and eastern europe: "16/17 + 1" cooperation as a tale of unfulfilled expectations. *Europe-Asia Studies*, 75(4): 583–605. https://doi.org/10.1080/09668136.2023.2179601.

Garlick, J., & Qin, F. (2023b). China's "do-as-I-do" paradigm: Practice-based normative diplomacy in the global South. *The Pacific Review*, 37(5): 985–1015. https://doi.org/10.1080/09512748.2023.2290619.

Gelfand, M. J., Raver, J. L., Nishii, L., et al. (2011). Differences between tight and loose cultures: A 33-nation study. *Science*, 332(6033): 1100–1104. https://doi.org/10.1126/science.1197754

Geyer, R., & Harrison, N. E. (2022). From order to complexity: The natural and social sciences. In Harrison, N. E., & Geyer, R. (eds.), *Governing Complexity in the 21st Century*. Abingdon: Routledge, pp. 14–32.

Giddens, A. (1984). *The Constitution of Society: Outline of the Theory of Structuration*. Cambridge: Polity.

Goldstein, J. S., & Pevehouse, J. C. (2014). *International Relations (10th ed.)*. Harlow: Pearson Education.

Graeber, D. (2004). *Fragments of an Anarchist Anthropology*. Chicago: Prickly Paradigm Press.

Gramsci, A. (1971). *Selections from the Prison Notebooks* (ed. & translated by Hoare, Q., & Smith, G. N.). New York: International.

Haidt, J. (2012). *The Righteous Mind: Why Good People are Divided by Politics and Religion*. London: Allen Lane.

Hare, B. (2017). Survival of the friendliest: *Homo sapiens* evolved via selection for prosociality. *Annual Review of Psychology*, 68: 1–32. https://doi.org/10.1146/annurev-psych-010416-044201.

Hare, B., Wobber, V., & Wrangham, R. (2012). The self-domestication hypothesis: Evolution of bonobo psychology is due to selection against aggression. *Animal Behaviour* 83: 573–585. https://doi.org/10.1016/j.anbehav.2011.12.007.

Hare, B., & Woods, V. (2020). *Survival of the Friendliest: Understanding Our Origins and Rediscovering Our Common Humanity*. New York: Random House.

Harrison, N. E. (ed.) (2006). *Complexity in World Politics: Concepts and Methods of a New Paradigm*. Albany: State University of New York Press.

Havercroft, J., & Prichard, A. (2017). Anarchy and international relations theory: A reconsideration. *Journal of International Political Theory*, 13(3): 252–265. https://doi.org/10.1177/1755088217719911.

Held, D. (1980). *Introduction to Critical Theory: Horkheimer to Habermas*. Berkeley: University of California Press.

Henrich, J. (2004). Cultural group selection, coevolutionary processes and large-scale cooperation. *Journal of Economic Behavior & Organization*, 53(1): 3–35. https://doi.org/10.1016/S0167-2681(03)00094-5.

Henrich, J. (2016). *The Secret of Our Success: How Culture is Driving Human Evolution, Domesticating Our Species, and Making Us Smarter*. Princeton: Princeton University Press.

Henrich, J. (2020) *The Weirdest People in the World: How the West Became Psychologically Peculiar and Particularly Prosperous*. New York: Farrar, Straus and Giroux.

Henrich, J, Heine, S. J., & Norenzayan, A. (2010). The weirdest people in the world? *Behavioral and Brain Sciences*, 33(2–3): 61–83. https://doi.org/10.1017/S0140525X0999152X.

Herrnstein, R. J. (1990). Rational choice theory: Necessary but not sufficient. *American Psychologist*, 45(3): 356–367. https://psycnet.apa.org/doi/10.1037/0003-066X.45.3.356.

Heying, H., & Weinstein, B. (2021). *A Hunter-Gatherer's Guide to the 21st Century: Evolution and the Challenges of Modern Life*. New York: Portfolio.

Hobson, J. M. (2004). *The Eastern Origins of Western Civilisation*. Cambridge: Cambridge University Press.

Hofstede, G., & Hofstede, G. J. (2005). *Cultures and Organizations: Software of the Mind*. New York: McGraw-Hill.

Holmes, M. (2014). International Politics at the Brain's Edge: Social Neuroscience and a New "Via Media." *International Studies Perspectives*, 15(2): 209–228. https://doi.org/10.1111/insp.12012.

Hui, V. T. (2005). *War and State Formation in Ancient China and Early Modern Europe*. Cambridge: Cambridge University Press.

Jackson, P. T., & Nexon, D. H. (2009). Paradigmatic faults in international-relations theory. *International Studies Quarterly*, 53(4): 907–930. https://doi.org/10.1111/j.1468-2478.2009.00562.x.

Jackson, R., & Sorensen, G. (2006). *Introduction to International Relations: Theories and Approaches* (3rd ed.). Oxford: Oxford University Press.

Jacobi, D., & Freyberg-Inan, A. (2015). Introduction: Human being(s) in international relations. In Jacobi, D., & Freyberg-Inan, A. (eds.), *Human Beings in International Relations*. Cambridge: Cambridge University Press, pp. 1–32.

Jervis, R. (1997). *System Effects: Complexity in Political and Social Life*. Princeton: Princeton University Press.

Kang, D. C. (2012). *East Asia before the West: Five Centuries of Trade and Tribute*. New York: Columbia University Press.

Kauffman, S. (1995). *At Home in the Universe: The Search for Laws of Self-Organization and Complexity*. London: Viking.

Kavalski, E. (2013). The struggle for recognition of normative powers: Normative power Europe and normative power China in context. *Cooperation and Conflict*, 48(2): 247–267. https://doi.org/10.1177/0010836713485386.

Kavalski, E. (2015). Complexifying IR: Disturbing the "deep Newtonian slumber" of the mainstream. In Kavalski, E. (ed.), *World Politics at the Edge of Chaos: Reflections on Complexity and Global Life*. Albany: State University of New York Press, pp. 253–272.

Keohane, R. O., & Nye, J. S. (1977). *Power and Interdependence: World Politics in Transition*. Boston: Little, Brown.

King, G., Keohane, R. O., & Verba, S. (1994). *Designing Social Inquiry: Scientific Inference in Qualitative Research*. Princeton: Princeton University Press.

Kinvall, C., & Mitzen, J. (2020). Anxiety, fear, and ontological security in world politics: Thinking with and beyond Giddens. *International Theory*, 12(2): 240–256. https://doi.org/10.1017/S175297192000010X.

Knutsen, T. L. (1997). *A History of International Relations Theory (2nd ed.)*. Manchester: Manchester University Press.

Krause, J., & Trappe, T. (2021). *A Short History of Humanity: A New History of Old Europe*. New York: Random House.

Kwan, A. S. C. (2016). Hierarchy, status and international society: China and the steppe nomads. *European Journal of International Relations*, 22(2): 362–383. https://doi.org/10.1177/1354066115598385.

Lacan, J. (2006). *Écrits: The First Complete Edition in English*, transl. by Fink, B. New York: W.W. Norton.

Laing, R. D. (1973). *The Divided Self*. Harmondsworth: Penguin.

Lakoff, G., & Johnson, M. (1980a). *Metaphors We Live By*. Chicago: University of Chicago Press.

Lakoff, G., & Johnson, M. (1980b). The Metaphorical Structure of the Human Conceptual System. *Cognitive Science*, 4: 195–208. https://doi.org/10.1207/s15516709cog0402_4.

Lebow, R. N. (2017). Evolution, adaptation, and imitation in international relations. *Oxford Research Encyclopedias, Politics*. https://doi.org/10.1093/acrefore/9780190228637.013.322.

Lederer, E. M. (2024). Russia vetoes a resolution calling for the prevention of a dangerous nuclear arms race in space. *The Associated Press*, 25 April. https://apnews.com/article/nuclear-arms-space-un-us-japan-russia-175d45ddb658729eff060bd8a83b8a55.

Lenin, V. I. (1999). *Imperialism, the Highest Stage of Capitalism*. Sydney: Resistance Books.

Lerner, J. S., Li, Y., Valdesolo, P., & Kassam, K. S. (2015). Emotion and decision making. *Annual Review of Psychology*, 66(1): 799–823. https://doi.org/10.1146/annurev-psych-010213-115043.

Longrich, N. R. (2019). Were other humans the first victims of the sixth mass extinction? *The Conversation*, 21 November. https://theconversation.com/were-other-humans-the-first-victims-of-the-sixth-mass-extinction-126638.

Lupovici, A. (2013). Me and the other in International Relations: An alternative pluralist International Relations 101. *International Studies Perspectives*, 14(3): 235–254. https://doi.org/10.1111/j.1528-3585.2012.00473.x.

Mahant, E. (2019). I've changed, I really have: Identity, regime change and ontological security. *Canadian Foreign Policy Journal*, 25(2): 188–202. https://doi.org/10.1080/11926422.2019.1571426.

Manners, I. (2002). Normative power Europe: A contradiction in terms? *Journal of Common Market Studies*, 40(2): 235–258. https://doi.org/10.1111/1468-5965.00353.

Marks, M. P. (2011). *Metaphors in International Relations Theory*. New York: Palgrave Macmillan.

Marks, M. P. (2018). *Revisiting Metaphors in International Relations Theory*. Cham: Palgrave Macmillan.

Mayseless, O. (2016). *The Caring Motivation: An Integrated Theory*. New York: Oxford University Press.

Mazzocchi, F. (2008). Complexity in biology: Exceeding the limits of reductionism and determinism using complexity theory. *EMBO Reports*, 9(1): 10–14. https://doi.org/10.1038/sj.embor.7401147.

McDermott, R., & Davenport, C. (2017). Toward an evolutionary theory of international relations. *Oxford Research Encyclopedias, Politics*. https://doi.org/10.1093/acrefore/9780190228637.013.294

Mearsheimer, J. J. (2001) *The Tragedy of Great Power Politics*. New York: Norton.

Milliken, J. (1999). The study of discourse in International Relations: A critique of research and method. *European Journal of International Relations*, 5(2): 225–254. https://doi.org/10.1177/1354066199005002003.

Mitzen, J. (2006). Ontological security in world politics: State identity and the security dilemma. *European Journal of International Relations*, 12(3): 341–370. https://doi.org/10.1177/1354066106067346.

Moore, G. J. (2020). *Niebuhrian International Relations: The Ethics of Foreign Policymaking*. New York: Oxford University Press.

Morgenthau, H. J. (1948). *Politics Among Nations: The Struggle for Power and Peace*. New York: Knopf.

Murray, M. (2019). *The Struggle for Recognition in International Relations: Status, Revisionism, and Rising Powers*. New York: Oxford University Press.

Muthukrishna, M., Doebeli, M., Chudek, M., & Henrich, J. (2018). The cultural brain hypothesis: How culture drives brain expansion, sociality, and life history. *PLoS Computational Biology*, 14: e1006504. https://doi.org/10.1371/journal.pcbi.1006504.

Neumann, I. B. (1996). Self and other in International Relations. *European Journal of International Relations*, 2(2): 139–174. https://doi.org/10.1177/1354066196002002001.

Niebuhr, R. (1941). *The Nature and Destiny of Man: A Christian Interpretation: Volume I: Human Nature*. New York: Charles Scribner's Sons.

Pagel, M. (2017). Q&A: What is human language, when did it evolve and why should we care? *BMC Biology*, 15, Article number 64. https://doi.org/10.1186/s12915-017-0405-3.

Paul, D. B. (2003). Darwin, social Darwinism and eugenics. In Hooge, J., & Radick, G. (eds.), *The Cambridge Companion to Darwin*. Cambridge: Cambridge University Press, pp. 214–239.

Penttinen, E. (2013). Posthumanism and feminist international relations. *Politics & Gender*, 9(1): 96–100. https://doi.org/10.1017/S1743923X12000736.

Prigogine, I., & Stengers, I. (1985). *Order out of Chaos: Man's New Dialogue with Nature*. London: Flamingo.

Rawls, J. (1971). *A Theory of Justice*. Cambridge, MA: Harvard University Press.

Reiter, D. (2015). Should we leave behind the subfield of international relations? *Annual Review of Political Science*, 18: 481–499. https://doi.org/10.1146/annurev-polisci-053013-041156.

Rennstich, J. K. (2018). Evolutionary systems theory: Concepts and schools in international relations. *Oxford Research Encyclopedias, International Studies*. https://doi.org/10.1093/acrefore/9780190846626.013.391.

Rosenberg, J. (1990). What's the matter with realism? *Review of International Studies*, 16(4): 285–303. https://doi.org/10.1017/S0260210500112379.

Schmidt, B. C., & Wight, C. (2023). Rationalism and the "rational actor assumption" in realist international relations theory. *Journal of International Political Theory*, 19(2): 158–182. https://doi.org/10.1177/17550882221144643.

Schuett, R. (2010). Classical realism, Freud and human nature in international relations. *History of the Human Sciences*, 23(2): 21–46. https://doi.org/10.1177/0952695110361421.

Sil, R., & Katzenstein, P. J. (2010). Analytic eclecticism in the study of world politics: Reconfiguring problems and mechanisms across research traditions. *Perspectives on Politics*, 8(2): 411–431. https://doi.org/10.1017/S1537592710001179.

Sil, R., & Katzenstein, P. J. (2011). *Beyond Paradigms: Analytic Eclecticism in the Study of World Politics*. Basingstoke: Palgrave Macmillan.

Snidal, D. (1985). The game theory of international politics. *World Politics*, 38(1): 25–57. https://doi.org/10.2307/2010350.

Steele, B. J. (2007). *Ontological Security in International Relations: Self-Identity and the IR State*. London: Routledge.

Sterling-Folker, J. (2001). Evolutionary tendencies in realist and liberal IR theory. In Thompson, R. W. (ed.), *Evolutionary Interpretations of World Politics*. Abingdon: Routledge, pp. 62–109.

Sterling-Folker, J. (2006). Lamarckian with a vengeance: Human nature and American International Relations theory. *Journal of International Relations and Development*, 9(3): 227–246. https://doi.org/10.1057/palgrave.jird.1800092.

Storr, W. (2021). *The Status Game: On Social Position and How We Use It*. London: William Collins.

Suntsova, M. V., & Buzdin, A. A. (2020). Differences between human and chimpanzee genomes and their implications in gene expression, protein functions and biochemical properties of the two species. *BMC Genomics*, 21 (Suppl 7): 535. https://doi.org/10.1186/s12864-020-06962-8.

Taleb, N. N. (2008) *The Black Swan: The Impact of the Highly Improbable*. London: Penguin.

Tang, S. (2013). *The Social Evolution of International Politics*. Oxford: Oxford University Press.

Tang, S. (2020). *On Social Evolution: Phenomenon and Paradigm*. Abingdon: Routledge.

Tannenwald, N. (2005). Ideas and explanation: Advancing the theoretical agenda. *Journal of Cold War Studies*, 7(2): 13-42. https://doi.org/10.1162/1520397053630619.

Tay, L., & Diener, E. (2011). Needs and subjective well-being around the world. *Journal of Personality and Social Psychology*, 101(2): 354–365. http://dx.doi.org/10.1037/a0023779.

Testot, L. (2020). *Cataclysms: An Environmental History of Humanity*. Chicago: University of Chicago Press.

Thompson, R. W. (ed.) (2001). *Evolutionary Interpretations of World Politics*. Abingdon: Routledge.

Turchin, P., Currie, T. E., Turner, E. A. L., & Gavrilets, S. (2013). War, space, and the evolution of old world complex societies. *Proceedings of the National Academy of Sciences of the United States of America*, 110(41): 16384–16389. https://doi.org/10.1073/pnas.1308825110.

Turchin, P., & Gavrilets, S. (2009). Evolution of complex hierarchical societies. *Social Evolution & History*, 8(2): 167–198. www.sociostudies.org/journal/articles/140588/.

Turner, J. H. (2021). *On Human Nature: The Biology and Sociology of What Made Us Human*. New York: Routledge.

Tuzin, D. (2001). *Social Complexity in the Making: A Case Study among the Arapesh of New Guinea*. London: Routledge.

van Gaal, S., De Lange, F. P., & Cohen, M. X. (2012). The role of consciousness in cognitive control and decision making. *Frontiers in Human Neuroscience*, 6: 121. https://doi.org/10.3389/fnhum.2012.00121.

Vince, G. (2019). *Transcendence: How Humans Evolved through Fire, Language, Beauty and Time*. London: Allen Lane.

Viotti, P. R., & Kauppi, M. V. (2001). *International Relations and World Politics: Security, Economy, Identity (2nd ed.)*. Upper Saddle River: Prentice-Hall.

Wæver, O. (1996). The rise and fall of the inter-paradigm debate. In Smith, S., Booth, K., & Zalewski, M. (eds.), *International Theory: Positivism and Beyond*. Cambridge: Cambridge University Press, pp. 149–185.

Waldrop, M. M. (1993). *Complexity: The Emerging Science at the Edge of Order and Chaos*. London: Viking.

Wallerstein, I. (1974). *The Modern World-System I: Capitalist Agriculture and the Origins of the European World-Economy in the Sixteenth Century*. New York: Academic Press.

Waltz, K.N. (1959). *Man, the State, and War: A Theoretical Analysis*. New York: Columbia University Press.

Waltz, K. N. (1979). *Theory of International Politics*. Reading: Addison-Wesley.

Waring, T. M., & Wood, Z. T. (2021). Long-term gene-culture co-evolution and the human evolutionary transition. *Proceedings of the Royal Society B: Biological Sciences*, 288: 20210538. https://doi.org/10.1098/rspb.2021.0538.

Wendt, A. (1992). Anarchy is what states make of it: The social construction of power politics. *International Organization*, 46(2): 391–425. https://doi.org/10.1017/S0020818300027764.

Wendt, A. (1999). *Social Theory of International Politics*. Cambridge: Cambridge University Press.

Wight, C. (1996). Incommensurability and cross-paradigm communication in international relations theory: "What's the frequency, Kenneth?" *Millennium: Journal of International Studies*, 22(2): 291–319. https://doi.org/10.1177/03058298960250020401.

Wilson, E. O. (2012). *The Social Conquest of Earth*. New York: Liveright.

Winston, C. (2018). Norm structure, diffusion, and evolution: A conceptual approach. *European Journal of International Relations*, 24(3): 638–661. https://doi.org/10.1177/1354066117720794.

Wrangham, R. (2019). *The Goodness Paradox*: *How Evolution Made Us More and Less Violent*. London: Profile Books.

Wrangham, R. W. (2009). *Catching Fire*: *How Cooking Made Us Human*. New York: Basic Books.

Wright, R. (1996). *The Moral Animal*: *Evolutionary Psychology and Everyday Life*. London: Abacus.

Wucker, M. (2016). *The Gray Rhino*: *How to Recognize and Act on the Obvious Dangers We Ignore*. New York: St Martin's Press.

Cambridge Elements

Applied Evolutionary Science

David F. Bjorklund
Florida Atlantic University

David F. Bjorklund is a Professor of Psychology at Florida Atlantic University in Boca Raton, Florida. He is the Editor-in-Chief of the *Journal of Experimental Child Psychology*, the Vice President of the Evolution Institute, and has written numerous articles and books on evolutionary developmental psychology, with a particular interest in the role of immaturity in evolution and development.

Editorial Board

David Buss, *University of Texas, Austin*
David Geary, *University of Missouri*
Mhairi Gibson, *University of Bristol*
Patricia Hawley, *Texas Tech University*
David Lancy, *Utah State University*
Jerome Lieberman, *Evolution Institute*
Todd Shackelford, *Oakland University*
Viviana Weeks-Shackelford, *Oakland University*
David Sloan Wilson, *SUNY Binghamton*
Nina Witoszek, *University of Oslo*
Rafael Wittek, *University of Groningen*

About the Series

This series presents original, concise, and authoritative reviews of key topics in applied evolutionary science. Highlighting how an evolutionary approach can be applied to real-world social issues, many Elements in this series will include findings from programs that have produced positive educational, social, economic, or behavioral benefits. Cambridge Elements in Applied Evolutionary Science is published in association with the Evolution Institute.

 THE EVOLUTION INSTITUTE

Cambridge Elements

Applied Evolutionary Science

Elements in the Series

Improving Breastfeeding Rates: Evolutionary Anthropological Insights for Public Health
Emily H. Emmott

The Hidden Talents Framework: Implications for Science, Policy, and Practice
Bruce J. Ellis, Laura S. Abrams, Ann S. Masten, Robert J. Sternberg, Nim Tottenham and Willem E. Frankenhuis

An Introduction to Positive Evolutionary Psychology
Glenn Geher, Megan Fritche, Avrey Goodwine, Julia Lombard, Kaitlyn Longo and Darcy Montana

Superorganism: Toward a New Social Contract for Our Endangered Species
Peter A. Corning

The Evolution of Reputation-Based Cooperation: A Goal Framing Theory of Gossip
Rafael Wittek and Francesca Giardini

Attachment and Parent-Offspring Conflict: Origins in Ancestral Contexts of Breastfeeding and Multiple Caregiving
Sybil L. Hart

The Evolved Mind and Modern Education: Status of Evolutionary Educational Psychology
David C. Geary

Evolutionary Perspectives on Enhancing the Quality of Life
Mads Larsen and Nina Witoszek

Evolution and the Fate of Humankind
Peter A. Corning

Evolution in International Relations
Jeremy Garlick

A full series listing is available at: www.cambridge.org/EAES

For EU product safety concerns, contact us at Calle de José Abascal, 56–1°, 28003 Madrid, Spain or eugpsr@cambridge.org.

www.ingramcontent.com/pod-product-compliance
Lightning Source LLC
LaVergne TN
LVHW020350260326
834688LV00045B/1647